BREAK THE NORMS

BREAK THE NORMS

QUESTIONING EVERYTHING YOU THINK
YOU KNOW ABOUT GOD AND TRUTH,
LIFE AND DEATH, LOVE AND SEX

CHANDRESH BHARDWAJ

sounds true
BOULDER, COLORADO

Sounds True
Boulder, CO 80306

Foreword © 2015 His Holiness the 14th Dalai Lama

Sounds True is a trademark of Sounds True, Inc.

Published 2015

Cover design by Rachael Murray
Book design by Beth Skelley

Printed in the United States of America

Library of Congress Cataloging-in-Publication Data
Bhardwaj, Chandresh.
  Break the norms : questioning everything you think you know about god and truth,
  life and death, love and sex / Chandresh Bhardwaj.
      pages cm
  ISBN 978-1-62203-541-0
  1. Thought and thinking. 2. Love. 3. Happiness. 4. Peace—Religious aspects.
  I. Title.
  BF441.B453 2015
  204—dc23
                                    2015015151

Ebook ISBN 978-1-62203-558-8

10 9 8 7 6 5 4 3 2 1

This book is to honor your life, **NAANI MAA.**
Thank you for your unconditional love.

To dear grandpa, **HIS HOLINESS SHREE RATTAN PINDORVI,**
for blessing me on the path of spirituality and poetry.

I bow down to the most important element
in my journey as I dedicate this book to my father,
HIS HOLINESS SHREE CHAMUNDA SWAMI,
for accepting me as his student and allowing me to be myself.

CONTENTS

FOREWORD

His Holiness the 14th Dalai Lama

Chandresh Bhardwaj belongs to a family of spiritual teachers and has a natural talent for spiritual matters. This book contains his vision on how to create love, peace, and happiness in our lives.

He has stressed in this book that knowing truth for oneself and not getting trapped by just what others or society says is key to attaining freedom and joy in life. This resonates with the Buddhist notion that liberation can be attained only through realizing truth, and that only truth can overcome suffering. What Chandresh says is true, because, generally, we are always carried away by short-term happinesses and social stereotypes—and we forget the need for inner values like love and compassion, which are the real foundations of our lives. As a result of that, we end up finding ourselves surrounded by misery and unhappiness. I am happy that Chandresh attempts to drive home these points to his readers.

I congratulate Chandresh for bringing out this book and for his innovative teaching style.

INTRODUCTION

BLINDLY FOLLOWING NORMS

I remember what it was like before I *really* knew the truth. Sure, I could recite Hindu scriptures from memory. I honored my family and my community, and pursued my culture's idea of "success" in my corporate finance job. It seemed like I was on a positive track. I was "comfortable." That's the goal, right? I thought I knew exactly what God wanted me to do—and I did my best to deliver.

But I often felt haunted inside. Deep down, I knew that I wasn't free. I felt like a robot, routinely thinking, acting, feeling, and behaving according to my programmer's desires. Have you ever felt this way?

Because I grew up in a family of spiritual Gurus, I spent my childhood studying with holy men and meditating in sacred temples. So I had the seeds of faith in my heart and these seeds grew into incredible spiritual experiences that made me feel deeply that I was not living up to my fullest potential. The intense meditations (*Sadhna*) had a message that echoed within my being: there was more to me that needed to unfold.

Spiritual teachings are borrowed knowledge. Our teachers and lineage holders can only point the way, and while we can absorb their messages, memorize sacred texts, and do the practices composed by enlightened beings, spirituality is meaningless if we only think about it, talk about it, and read about it. Only after experiencing those teachings in our day-to-day lives do we become *spiritual*.

What I realized was that I needed to leave my conditioning behind in order to experience the real me. I had often heard that a divine

1

presence within could dissolve all limiting patterns and lead me to a life of freedom—but I had not yet had a concrete experience of this truth. I knew I had to break my norms, rooted deep down in my soul. I had to move beyond my culture's idea of success and God. Continually, I have to write my own success story and find the God who speaks to me directly, not through pundits and priests.

I can't say there was one dramatic moment in which I suddenly "woke up" and realized that I was free to break out of the conditioning that ran my life. There were many spiritual experiences to remind me of my purpose as I grew up. I would often listen, but passively, without acting on them because the courage to walk my talk was still missing. Part of me wanted to continue the comfortable life that we all are conditioned to pursue—while another part constantly felt the spiritual pull to lead a movement to raise human awareness. It was a tug of war.

It was the deaths of my sister and a childhood friend that planted the seeds of questioning in me. Their lives ended, but mine started to expand—and I was left alone to guide my fate. My sister was a bright student who was very well versed in mantras. When she started falling ill, I never thought the sickness would end in her death. My mind constantly reaffirmed to me that young people don't die of sickness. Why would anything bad happen to her?

My dad called one day while I was visiting and asked my sister to recite the *Kujjika*, a two-page Sanskrit mantra. She recited it all in one breath. She always did. The significance in this recitation was that it was her last one. My sister slipped into a coma right after saying the last word. We lost her a few days later.

This tragedy changed me forever. To work with my grief, I started meditating for hours, even days. But there was something more waiting to test my strength. Just three years later, I lost my best friend in a sudden accident. I heard the news in my basement room, and my soul was so shocked that I couldn't sleep in that room for more than a month.

Their passings opened up all my questions about life and death, about meaning and how to live. I thought I knew the answers to it all. But I feel they left an assignment for me to complete. Over time, I would come to understand that my life's work is not about finding the answers to my questions—it is about building the courage to question my answers. But I had to pursue false answers before I learned to truly question.

In 2004, I left India to join my father in New York City and pursue a business degree. I attended one of the best colleges with the full intention of working in the finance industry until I turned forty years old. Only then would I establish a spiritual center where I could impart all my spiritual practice to people who wish to adopt a mindful lifestyle. But within a year of landing an internship at an investment-banking firm, the chaos I witnessed in New York inspired me to leave the financial world.

It was not just the blind race after money that bothered me. It was a painful feeling of being enslaved by the conditioning to be the "best." Being myself wasn't an option. I was expected to be the fastest rat in the rat race. Thankfully, a mentor helped me find the courage to take a look at my genuine self.

During my sophomore year in college, Maureen Berrios, a smart and successful CPA, hired me for tax season. I watched her shower tough love on every intern but me. To make sure I was not invisible to her—and not just a dumb intern—I asked her a question one evening.

"Maureen, how am I doing? A little feedback will help me to improve."

She gazed into my eyes like a tough but caring mother as she said, "Are you ready to hear the truth?" I pretended that I was ready. She poured it all out in one breath: "I don't think this is the place for you. I don't mean this office, specifically. I mean Wall Street, the material world. You are meant to help the world by adding meaning to our lives. Your energy is so different from all the people I come across. You can decide to stay in the financial industry. But ultimately, you will be on a social service path helping people with your wisdom."

Maureen was so confident about this that when I requested that she write a recommendation letter for my MBA application to Harvard, she said, "Let them come to study under you. Why are you going there?" Attending Harvard was the dream I had set my heart on when I left India. I wanted to be a Harvard MBA graduate. So when Maureen said *they will come to you,* I thought either she was consoling me because I wasn't a fit for Harvard yet or she really did see something in me.

Her words eventually led me to see in myself what she saw. I left the financial industry and started Break the Norms as a platform to help spiritual seekers. And one of my first clients was from Harvard. I even took a few Harvard alumni to India for a spiritual retreat. Maureen knew.

Life changed gradually as I started to peel off the layers that society had tattooed upon me. I began to understand that spirituality is a daily job. If we apply ourselves diligently, with regularity, to our meditation and learning, we will glimpse, little by little, the divine truth within. This is the key to freedom: We must experience divine truth for ourselves. Any good teacher will only guide us to awaken what already exists inside.

As a student of divine light and a seventh-generation spiritual teacher, I've dedicated my life to spreading this message to the seekers globally. I am committed to living a free, fearless life and helping others to do the same. I have decided to walk in each and every corner of the world and pick the seekers who are willing to live this spiritual path. The freedom and clarity that I have discovered in me is meant to be in the lives of everyone.

Growing up in a household of Gurus, I have been exposed to hundreds of spiritual paths. The approach that resonates for me the most is Tantra. Most of my communication in this book comes from a Tantric perspective.

Now, I know what you may be thinking: *Isn't Tantra all about sex?*

The short answer is no. Tantra is a full tradition, rich in wisdom, myth, sacred texts, practices, and revelations. It makes me sad to see websites claiming to offer "mind-blowing sex with Tantra." This kind of thing gives Tantra a bad rep. People think Tantra is Indian pornography, or complicated acrobatics for the bedroom. The irony is that Tantra certainly can blow your mind, but not in a pornographic way!

Originating in India, Tantra emerged as a response to the ascetic, monastic traditions of renunciation that filled the land. Before the development of Tantra, the most common way to walk a spiritual path was to leave your home, family, and profession. It meant going to meditate in a monastery or cave, shaving your head and wearing robes, and often begging for food at the temple. The idea was that the only way to fully experience spirit was to separate yourself from the distractions of sexuality, lust, career, business, greed—all worldly attachments. Only then could the mind become quiet enough, and pure enough, to see God.

While these older Indian traditions recommend that seekers remove themselves from the trappings of a human life in favor of a monastic path, Tantra teaches enlightenment within a typical human life. It is taught for householders who have homes, marriages, families, jobs, and responsibilities. Tantra wants us to achieve the best of both the spiritual and material worlds. It wants us to experience the sacred right in our daily lives. That's why it includes topics considered taboo in other religions, like sex and money. Tantra evolved from older traditions to benefit those who wanted both spiritual and worldly success. Always immensely practical, Tantra offers philosophies and technologies to support seekers in realizing their divine nature—while staying in the world of intimate relationships, family, livelihood, and all the messiness that comes with human life.

Some Tantric teachings *do* address sexuality. That's so those who do not choose celibacy can learn to work with their sexual energy as divine energy—to have a transcendent experience in their bodies. Have you heard of the chakras? That entire system of energetic centers in the body originates in Tantric tradition. We call this system the "subtle body."

By associating Tantra exclusively with sex, the Western world has corrupted what began as a pure and powerful method for working with the subtle body. Tantra invites us to experience ecstatic states of healing and transcendence in our own bodies and in connection with others.

Today, it is more important than ever to understand Tantra. The essence of Tantra lies in its strength to make you spiritually independent. Tantra teaches each of us to accept and acknowledge ourselves the way we are. In fully accepting the totality of our embodied experience, we can access the freedom that is our birthright.

Tantric teachings are based on the notion that truth is not reliant on conditions. That means the divine can be found *through* our humanity. While other traditions teach that we must banish sexual desires, anger, greed, ego, and many other "negative" emotions, Tantra invites us to use each human experience as a pathway to our higher selves. And that's the intention of this book, too.

I teach Tantric practices and principles because they make sense to me—and because they *work*. But everything I say can be applied to your life, regardless of religion or creed. Please embrace or reject whatever I say on your own terms. If Tantra resonates with you, that's great. If not, you will find some spiritual perspective that makes sense to you. All true spiritual paths lead to the same place. The key is finding one that feeds your unique soul.

As you engage this path, get ready to be brutally honest. Get ready to unlearn your suffering. It's time to discover our real reasons for being alive. It's time to break the norms. I want you to know that you will not find a formula in this book. I do not have a "one size fits all" prescription to yield specific results for every single person. I will not give you a map of where to go in your life. But I *will* give you instruments for your travel. I will share stories, teachings, and tools that invite you to see your own true nature for yourself. It's that nature that is your guide. It's that infinitely intelligent space in you that will illuminate your path.

When you read this book, you can expect to be challenged. I am not here to fluff up your concepts of who you think you are. I am not here to tell you that you are beautiful and perfect just as you are, and that you can have everything you dream of no matter what. If that's what you're after, you'll have to find a different book!

I'm here to point you toward something much deeper and more important than that. I'm here to expose your blind spots so that you can bring them into your direct vision. It's those blind spots—those subjects our psyches have made taboo—which block our connection to the Source.

While we uncover blind spots, we can expect some cosmic punches. We are programmed to crave cosmic blessings. A cosmic punch is similar to what your mom gave you when you wouldn't stop eating cookies. It is tough love to improve your life. It is needed because the structures that have kept our lives in place may need to fall away. Relationships may need to end. We may need to be humbled. Jobs may take on whole new forms.

But I promise, the clarity and freedom that comes with the discovery at hand is worth any growing pains you may encounter along the way.

The information I am going to share with you in this book is special and sacred. I have come across many who are in the market to check out new spiritual teachings for weekend reading. But this book is not for lazy weekend reading. Read even just a page or two daily, but do it with your whole awareness involved. Bring everything deeper into your experience by writing down the questions and thoughts that pop up in your mind during the reading. Then you can refer to, savor, and reflect on them over and over again.

In chapter 1, I will start with an overview of what it means to break the norms and take a first look at how to do it. Each subsequent chapter will focus on one specific (and often taboo) area of life. In each area, I will illuminate cultural norms that widely influence our beliefs about the world and, therefore, deserve a thorough investigation. I will share my perspective on each norm and invite you to question each norm for yourself.

The exercises and meditations in each chapter are meant to support you in your process of discovering the truth for yourself. They will help you to take what you've read beyond the realm of the mind and into a deeper place in your soul. Take the time to do the exercises so you can receive the maximum benefits of this book.

My hope is that this book will be a mirror for your life. I want to hold the mirror in such a way that you can see directly into the cycles of pain and suffering that you unconsciously repeat. With this kind of reflection, you can take steps to create powerful change. My intention is to reflect your own wisdom back to you, so you can see it and claim it for yourself. I will be doing a very poor job if, years from today, my students are still making appointments to see me for the same problems they came for five years ago. My aim is to make you independent of me and, at heart, independent of every spiritual Guru out there. It will not happen overnight, but it *will* happen. I want to be there for you as a guide.

You are a precious human with incredible talents. There is no one "out there" who can claim what is yours to discover. I want to witness the splendor of freedom in your eyes. I want to ignite your divine spark into a sacred fire that burns through your conditioned consciousness. You *can* embrace a new awareness—a higher one—and this book will help you get there.

THE UNLEARNING
BEGINS

Too many souls suffer the disillusionment that comes from following a destiny that is not their own. Instead of waking up joyful and energized, many of us feel like robots, pushing forward like a machine to keep life going. We feel trapped by our commitments and lost without material things we believe we must have. We struggle to behave in ways that are respectable and work to arrive at what we think we should achieve.

We follow paths that are "normal" in our culture. I call these external patterns that shape our lives "norms." My definition of a *norm* is "any thought or behavior that has been learned from outside sources, such as parents, religion, culture, or society at large." Norms may or may not reflect our internal truths, but most of us don't take the time to notice how they fit. Instead, we blindly follow a norm laid before us by others—a path that always leads to a dead end. This is because if we never examine these norms that influence our choices, we may have a persistent, haunted feeling. We may suffer with anxiety or feel lost. To distract ourselves from this harrowing emptiness, we may drink more alcohol or get hooked on reality TV. Maybe we'll seek fulfillment by going to one self-help workshop after another or following strict diets. Or perhaps we'll try to find an idealized romantic relationship or dream of the freedoms we'd have by leaving the relationship we are in. In so many ways, we look outside ourselves for the fulfillment we wish we could find inside.

And what if we *do* look deeper, only to discover we feel culturally "unacceptable" emotions like anger or sexual urges? We may try to hide or suppress these feelings in order to maintain our sense of stability. But instead, they come out in ways that make us feel crazy. We look at the long line in the grocery store and want to push people out of our way, or we find it painful to sit in the car while traffic moves at five miles per hour. We might become addicted to pornography, or even want to participate in sexual violence.

Perhaps the saddest outcome from blindly following the norms is a feeling that life is passing us by. We know we are not exactly *happy*, but we have no idea how to make changes. We have heard of this nice thing called "purpose," and while we might want that for ourselves, we think that kind of spiritual insight is only for bestselling authors or famous philanthropists or people living in caves. We may even lie awake at night fearing death. Or worse, fearing that we haven't ever really lived.

We have no tools to understand our divinity. We hear about it, read about it, but are too afraid to explore it. It feels too weird to ask questions, either of ourselves or of others, about topics that baffle us—questions like, "What happens when we die?" "Will I ever find my soul mate?" and "Is there a God?" These are some of the taboo questions that we will explore in this book. If we don't address these questions, we will continue to suffer in silence, or ignore that we have a problem, or even blame external factors for our pain. If we blame our parents, God, our karma, or our partners, we're still turning our awareness outside of ourselves—and distancing ourselves even further from what we truly seek. We may even reject the help of a sincere spiritual teacher.

We simply don't realize there is another way.

BREAKING THE NORMS

To outsiders, it looks like Adam has it all—a lovely home in Los Angeles, an attractive wife, two darling children, a glamorous car, and a hearty reserve of wealth. As the head of a reputed media-consulting firm, meeting the who's who of Hollywood is just another day. But Adam looks at his life and wonders, "Is this all there is?" He has been drinking an extra scotch or two each night to "take the edge off" after a long day. Sometimes he wakes up in the middle of the night in a cold sweat, but he can't quite figure out why.

It's time to call bullshit on the cultural programming that keeps us enslaved to external influences. It's time to question taboo subjects for ourselves. How we can do that is what this book is all about.

I want you to know that you can completely overhaul your life. Whatever is not working can shift into something new. It takes a strong commitment on your part, and it won't be easy—but it can happen. You can upgrade your quality of life, on your terms. You can function at a higher level that is fueled by inspiration. And you can free yourself to follow your deepest passions. How to do this is as simple as questioning the norms for yourself—and discovering the free soul that lives in your heart.

Each of us has a shining, resilient, infinitely intelligent soul. Life's conditions sometimes beat us down and make us forget our true nature. These conditions could be pressure to get good grades in school, the struggle to survive the rat race, or the compulsion to follow the status quo. We can get trapped inside the demands that come from outside ourselves. These demands could be from a spouse who feels you don't care for their feelings, a boss who feels you are a burden on the company, or an investment that you owned but now owns you. Conditionings may have built a home in us. And that home can be quite sturdy. My entire practice focuses on shaking these "homes" built in us.

When we clear the cultural and familiar dross that covers our light, a new life becomes possible. We can see through the external conditioning planted in us by society, religion, and the media, to name a few. The good news is that we don't need a figure from heaven to help us see through our patterns. A daily disciplined practice of meditation will help us to sail through this journey. In addition to meditation, be willing to listen to the truth. Speaking the truth is great, but listening to the truth with no guards is liberating.

This openness to truth helps us to make conscious choices. Human beings are blessed with the gift of choice every day. The daily conscious choices we make will determine if we react to our patterns or take a stand to end these patterns forever. Breaking the norms is a daily task to say "Yes" to our inner awareness and "No" to external judgments and demands. We turn down the noise and turn up the refreshing silence that guides us. That's what it means to break the norms.

If we can do this, taboo subjects like death and sex will no longer confuse us, because we have examined them for ourselves. I must add, however, that examination won't be easy. I remember when I started my practice as a spiritual advisor, I would greet all my students and clients by saying, "Please, make yourself comfortable!" Soon, I realized that my job was not about making anyone comfortable. If I make you comfortable, I am simply feeding your ego. A thorough examination of the soul always involves asking tough questions, sweeping away the dirt, and rewriting your life story. None of us is ever ready to do it. We are never taught to be vulnerable and naked with our souls. And that's exactly why it gets so tough and so messy.

But the result of this examination is a renewed you. You will experience clarity in your intention and understand the value of your existence. Just to practice now for a quick moment, take a deep breath, watch your eyes in a mirror or even in your smartphone camera, and say to yourself, "I am ready to build my life around love and fearlessness. I will do all that it takes to clear the obstacles in my life." Make sure you say this while gazing deeply into your eyes. It does have a magical effect.

We can embrace our humanness with skill and acceptance—challenges and all. We, as humans, are gifted with many powers. The power to evolve our awareness is my personal favorite. I believe that's what makes us human. Otherwise, what are we? Robots? Or rats in the lab experimented on by others? We constantly revolve around the circus of life. It is our humanness that separates us from human "doing" and makes us human "beings." The humanness slows our minds down and makes space for spiritually enriching potential.

We can see clearly and, therefore, make good choices for ourselves. Before we question what we've been taught, our vision is blurred by endless instructions we are given to follow. I was watching one of the episodes of *Orange Is the New Black* where a senior officer instructs a junior officer to call inmates "inmate" instead of by their names. This practice makes the inmates feel they are not human, not part of a normal group. Our everyday reality isn't far from this scenario: traditions that are simply passed on to us can make us feel like prisoners or cattle. The sickness of conditioning is at the level that it feels "normal" to be part of the crowd. Anything else feels odd and awkward. That's why questioning norms can feel confusing or more complex—at first.

Leaders like Gandhi and Martin Luther King Jr. created upheaval initially. That's because their questioning broke the status quo and caused their followers to wake up from the accepted crowd mentality. But eventually their questions became a route of their own. And these days, their teachings are incredibly clear and liberating. The same is true for us. Understanding that some work needs to be done and having the courage to take a step toward it every day is what really makes things clearer.

We can go from acting like robots to acting like dignified human beings.

To go from norm-follower to truth-follower is a revolutionary change. It is like being fed food that causes you heartburn for twenty years, and then finally being fed the most delicious, nourishing meal you've ever had, as if it were prepared just for your digestive needs. It gets even better when you realize you can eat like that every single day!

When we follow our truth, we feel excited each morning. When we don't, our moods and reactions often get tied up with situations around us. The situation could be anything, but we don't need to make it our personal problem. A person overtaking you on a highway and crossing in front of you while honking is making *himself* trouble. Don't take it personally. If a woman at the cash counter of your grocery store is a bit cold, let her be; it has nothing to do with you. Our spouses have a world of their own, just as we do, and it's okay to let them be in it at times. It's okay to live in a state of freedom and allow others to do the same. As a result, we will feel pleased with how we are shaping our lives. Even though we can't completely escape pain, we won't struggle so much and we become resilient.

By indulging in the daily drama of life, we go far, far away from the truth of life. Krishnamurti, the Indian philosopher, always said that truth is a pathless land. No one has a monopoly on it. It evolves as our awareness evolves.

THE TRUTH BEYOND THE TRICKS

Susan is not my wife!

Susan is not my wife!

Susan is not my wife!

Can you imagine those words as a mantra for a happy and spicy married life? Well, they are. Let me explain.

My client Mark was married to Susan, but he wasn't doing a very good job of being a husband. He ignored his family commitments and kept a cold distance from everyone around him. Because his world felt painful and empty, Mark was also experimenting with various forms of pleasure. He was trying drugs, sex, and anything else he could find that would disconnect him from his feelings. But this left him plagued by an endless cycle of guilt, shame, and fear that he did not want to even begin facing—much less the void that had grown within him.

Before coming to me, Mark went to a therapist. With guilt and pain, he told the therapist, "I don't feel attracted to my wife anymore! I just don't."

Mark's therapist suggested that Mark was not attracted to Susan for one reason: because she was his wife. According to the therapist, "Men get bored with their wives. You have to forget that she's your wife." The prescription? You guessed it: every day, say, "Susan is not my wife."

Mark said this "mantra" religiously—while taking a shower, while driving, and whenever he got a moment. The mind starts to believe the lies that we tell it. It doesn't take too long for the mind to accept any belief that we feed it. Mark was almost addicted to repeating this "mantra," and it kept him in a fantasy world. Soon after, Mark started feeling that Susan was really not his wife—that she was a desirable woman who he could fantasize about. Mark started looking at Susan as a woman who exists to satisfy his fantasies.

But somehow, the new "mantra" did not help Mark. Or Susan.

Instead of getting to the roots of his suffering, Mark was stuck in an endless loop of trying to manage, control, and even trick his mind. The problem with the therapist's approach was that while she did offer a surface-level fix, she did not direct Mark to look into his own heart and ask hard questions—questions like, "What am I really looking for when

I have sex?" "Why am I feeling pain?" "What can bring me feelings of pleasure?" and "What is missing from my life?" Since he did not understand where his self-sabotaging thoughts and habits originated, he could not get to the roots of his suffering. He never examined the effects his family, religion, and culture had on his consciousness. He continued to avoid facing taboo subjects like sex and love.

As a result, Mark continued to act out his confusing desires, which came out in harmful ways—including an addiction to sex. He indulged in affairs outside of his marriage. Soon it became a habit for him. He was often angry and would react loudly to even minor things. Using drugs and alcohol was draining his creativity and energy. He was losing touch with reality, because his actions only yielded more misery in himself and others—but he couldn't figure out why. When Mark came to me, he was not living the life of fulfillment and gratitude that is possible for all of us. His life had no purpose, no meaning, and no joy. In Mark's cluttered mind, there was no room for any spark of the divine.

Often, when we try to find relief from pains caused by impulsive, destructive behavior, this kind of thing happens. We look for a teacher or therapist to help us, but the techniques we hear do not lead to true and lasting change—mostly because they come from outside us. We do not find healing, so we decide that we cannot feel happy in our lives. Maybe others can find happiness. But not us.

UNLEARN THE WAYS YOU WERE TAUGHT TO SUFFER

Breaking the norms is not about learning how to trick your mind. It's not about acting in a different way, hoping for a better outcome. And it's certainly not a list of "how to become enlightened in ten days." Until we actually engage our own minds and hearts to question the norms that dictate our own lives, we will only go from one shallow prescription to the next. We will keep looking to "experts" to solve our problems. Although we may learn techniques to manage our craziness, we will never really get to experience our true potential.

Breaking the norms is about unlearning whatever we have been taught and unlearning whatever is not true for us. Our "problems" are anything that keeps us from living a clear, authentic life. It could be as pervasive as an addiction, or as subtle as a belief that we have no time to meditate even though we know it is good for us. Breaking the norms is about unraveling the grip our families and cultures have on our hearts. Only then can we wake up and say, "My life is precious. I deserve to liberate myself from all the conditioning. I am ready to see the ways I have taken on norms that hold me back. I am ready to live as I am meant to live."

When we break our attention away from striving to make our lives and selves appear a certain way, our life force frees up. We can use that life force to understand our problems from their source. Breaking the norms gives us crystal clear vision into the roots of our suffering.

When Mark came to me, he had never looked at the norms behind his troublesome behavior. But by asking the hard questions, he came to understand that his beliefs about his relationship with his wife were colored by his own father's infidelity. His father had a life filled with wealth and fame. Mark had often seen him being overly close with other ladies and overly angry with Mark's mother. The dysfunction in the family had rooted fear in him about love and relationships. In Catholic school, he was taught that sex was shameful, but at the same time, he lived in a town with countless billboards selling sex. At every other corner, there was a strip club ready to give "pleasure" for a few bucks. He was very confused!

When things don't go as we plan in life, we start to look for distractions or solutions. Mark was distracted by his search for solutions. The dysfunctional family experiences, school teachings, and L.A. strip clubs were not making sense to his mind. Mark was not an utterly irresponsible or insensitive person. If he were, he wouldn't have agreed to follow my guidelines. He was an emotional being strangled between what-should and what-is. His mind would tell him to do one thing, but his awareness (which had gone all awry) would point to some other direction. He read spiritual bestsellers but started feeling they were too clichéd and boring.

Has that ever happened to you? You want to change but don't find that one voice to follow? Mark was on a similar path. His confusion and questions were motivating him to change. He was aware enough to understand that the path he was on would not end well.

As he questioned all of these aspects of his "normal" life, Mark gained greater clarity into what he really wanted—a nourishing relationship with Susan. He wanted more than sexual fulfillment, more than the fantasy he had been chasing in his wife. He wanted to connect with her intimately. But even more than that, he wanted a fulfilling relationship with *himself*. Now Susan and Mark meditate together every night. Their relationship is healing, and they're both happier.

Unlearning is the first step to *dissolving* our problems. Otherwise, we're just making different problems. When we actually dissolve the issues, God can come rushing into the space we have made. We can be free to follow our truth. Letting problems dissolve comes from a state of choiceless awareness. In this state—which we access by telling the truth—our troublesome habits and useless thoughts lose their power. When we feed our souls with the truth, we starve our conditioning. That's because conditioning survives only when there is confusion, doubt, and fear. But our awareness of truth edges out all of the energies that keep conditioning alive. So our problems get sick, slow down, and eventually die. At a minimum, we learn to see troublesome thoughts and ignore them instead of letting them influence our behavior.

I hope you won't be confused between dissolving your problems and suppressing them. Suppressing problems comes from what I call a "shrunken awareness." Most of us are tied in to the drama of life. This results in either running away from problems or simply hiding them in a box. Our biggest addiction is not coffee, cigarettes, or any other substance. Our biggest addiction is constantly overanalyzing our problems. While it's good to be aware of our problems, magnifying them through the lens of shrunken awareness leads only to misery.

The process of unlearning starts from a willingness to change no matter what. You have to be ready to go back to the source of your conditioning. No one says it will be easy! But it will be worth it. You will likely find the roots of problems in your education, religion, and the society in which you grew up. All these elements now have a home in your consciousness. It will be tough, almost painful, to move away from them. But the process needs to happen in order to take care of the problems from the roots themselves. The process will be slow but organic. You cannot make this happen by force. You didn't come to this world by force. You stayed in the cozy womb for nine months or so and then grew little by little every day. The dissolving of your conditioning will also happen little by little.

Here are a few questions that I want you to keep asking until your mind stops talking and your soul starts answering:

- What has been my deepest desire?
- What have I learned in my education?
- What is my instant reaction to stress and pain?
- What do I do to solve my problems?
- Do I trust my heart?
- Do I have compassion for my own journey?
- What was the last mistake that I made? What caused me to choose the actions that led to this mistake? What's my lesson?

Asking these questions daily will help you understand your problematic areas. Don't worry about finding the right answers. You'll know you're on the right track when you start observing these changes within you:

- A fearless attitude toward your goals
- A better grip on how problems operate
- An understanding of your stress
- Fewer reactions and more responses to life's challenges
- Better connection with your emotions
- The freedom to be yourself
- More courage to express your voice on opinions that matter to you

I will leave the rest of the results for you to share with me.

UNLEARNING UNCOVERS YOUR PURPOSE

When we unlearn the norms, we can truly accept the gift of our life. We are not here by accident. We are each here to fulfill a unique purpose, to contribute to the world in a unique way. And what really makes us happy, what really feels *true,* is the only indication that we are on the right track. We don't have time to waste on anything else.

In India, they say that a soul must live eighty-four thousand lives before it can incarnate as a human. A human birth is considered a most auspicious blessing. Now, I have no idea whether that's true, and I don't claim to know exactly what happens after death. But I do agree that a human life is a tremendous opportunity, a wondrous phenomenon not to be wasted.

Through some mysterious, miraculous process, the infinite energy of life itself has taken form as you and me. Let's discuss this for a moment to really take that in. It's easy to get wrapped up in the demands of life and forget that, despite its problems, life is a miraculous gift. Ask yourself this question: "Is it a miracle to exist?"

If you are really quiet and really honest, don't you think so? We have the opportunity to stare at an ocean and feel awe. We can look into the eyes of our beloved, or a child, and be knocked over by love. We can crumble with full-body laughter and forget everything but pure joy. Any way you might experience awe points to life as an amazing thing.

Unlearning external norms means you can finally learn about this amazing self. Some people have liberated themselves by quitting jobs they hate but that they took to pay for fancy houses that society makes a status symbol. Other people have committed to relationships with people they love even though their families think the relationships are inappropriate. Whatever the result of your liberation, you finally have insight into what makes your heart tick. And you will have the courage to follow whatever your heart reveals to you. Life can be rich with meaning and fulfillment.

Stress comes from trying to gain something you don't really want in the first place. When you are aligned with your purpose, you will feel refreshed, relaxed, and energized by your daily life.

WHATEVER YOU SEE, SEE IT WITH AWARENESS

There is one thing that separates a norm-breaker from the rest of the crowd: awareness. Awareness, as I define it, is staying fully present and witnessing yourself in each moment, without judgment. This book shows you how to apply awareness to reaching your truth.

Awareness is the first step to breaking your norms. Whatever you see, see it with awareness. Don't assume, and don't generalize. Just be with whatever you are experiencing without trying to change it. Put your awareness into every act, every moment. Feel the hot shower, evening breeze, food, water, human touch, sky, people on the road—all that surrounds you.

At times, you will feel bombarded with all the emotions and energies around you. How you deal with your daily emotions will have a major impact on your relationship with your awareness. It won't be possible to be a Buddha 24/7, but it will become possible if you stay consistent with your intention to access your awareness.

I recommend adding an intention to be in touch with your awareness. This will make the process smoother. A meditation with a right intention has miraculous effects. While you choose to be in touch with your awareness, don't fight against your emotions. I want you to laugh and cry as a natural flow of your lifestyle. There will be days when you feel like you have no idea what you are doing with your life. Be okay with the contradictory messages within. These mixed messages will rise when you start sweeping the dirt away. It's important to notice the feelings without judging them, and to let them come and go. There will be conflicting desires—simply acknowledge all of them and be patient.

A baby offers a great example of how to practice awareness without judgment. When a baby feels hungry, he cries for food. One moment he may want to be held, and the next moment he may want to be in his crib. He does not weigh in on whether his desires are acceptable. He does not stress over what they mean for his future. He does not know how to censor himself—that is, until adults teach him to care what they think. It is beneficial to be in a childlike state while learning to be aware.

The more you add your awareness in life, the more meaning you will add to your existence. You will start responding. You will start to matter to life. You will start to see life in ways that never happened before.

The biggest bonanza of this process is your enriched relationship with yourself. You will grow to accept your flaws in a nonjudgmental manner.

The struggle to fit in will cease. We try to fit in because we think we need validation from groups. We have been told clearly that we need to be something awesome, something better, in order to have an acceptable social circle and be successful. In a state of self-awareness, you will stop chasing the perfect image. The judgments of others will not haunt your nights. You will finally rise up to your true potential.

A norm-breaker cannot take her spiritual path casually. As you start to break through your conditioning, you will feel powerful and wise. Don't take this power for granted. You will be fulfilled with the power of manifesting life on your own terms. What it means for you is that you have to create your life with a commitment to humility. You have to lead others by example. Walk your talk on the spiritual path. Continue to contemplate your life, your loved ones, and everyone you come across. Seeing you breaking your norms, people will want to follow your lead. Be an example. Lead them responsibly, and make sure to take good care of yourself along the way.

For example, eat well. In the Ayurvedic tradition, they say, "You are what you eat," and I fully stand by that phrase. Food emits energy, so eat food that emits good energy. You need your physical body to decode the potential of your soul. So nurture it well!

And perhaps most important, remember to question everything. Many seekers want to apply their knowledge and become teachers too quickly. Don't be in a rush. This book is not a yoga certification course that will grant you a title in three months. To be a norm-breaker is a lifetime process. My father, a renowned spiritual Guru, starts every talk with one line: *I am a most ignorant student of spirituality.* Never stop learning. A soldier fights. A musician composes. And a seeker seeks—every day, in every way possible.

EXERCISE **UNCOVER YOUR CURRENT PERSPECTIVE**

This exercise gives you the chance to take inventory of your beliefs about the current state of your life. It will reveal the overarching beliefs that hold you back. Then, it will show you what you really want, but think is impossible. Do this exercise now, before you read the rest of the book. Then, after you have spent some time exploring and integrating the lessons in this book, come back and do it again. Compare how your lists have changed.

In your journal, make a list of seven things you would like to be different about your life. If you could wave your magic wand, what would appear? What would disappear? Don't censor yourself, and don't worry about whether these desires seem attainable or not. Simply ask yourself: How would my life be different if it could be? For example, you might want to leave your corporate job and become an artist.

Now, go back to your list and write two positive changes you would see in your life if you magically attained each desire. In the example, you would be happier. You would also feel like you were living your true purpose.

Then, write down two negative changes that might happen as well. On the negative side of the example, you might struggle with money and you might disappoint your parents.

Now, go back over the list one more time. Notice what dreams and habits emerged out of this exercise and write down both the positive and negative sides. The positive changes are your dreams. Using the example, you might dream of being your own boss, living your purpose, and expressing yourself fearlessly. The negative changes are the current habits that are holding you back. These could be fear about criticism, marketing your work, or being rejected.

Asking yourself these deep questions helps you get to the bottom of why you are where you are in your life. The rest of this book will help you discover your deeper awareness and help you to live your purpose.

UNCENSORED SPIRITUALITY

2

Imagine that you're invited to a glamorous party in your town. Everyone will be wearing their nicest clothing, and you don't want to be the odd one out. But you don't feel like you have the right clothes to garner everyone's attention, so you decide to borrow someone else's shirt and wear it to the party. At the party, you get compliments, gain high regard and everyone's attention because of the shirt you're wearing. You feel special. Everything is going well until the person who loaned you the shirt shows up and asks for it back. You plead with him to let you keep wearing the shirt until the party is over, but nothing works. He strips the shirt off you and walks out of the party. You're left shirtless, embarrassed, and angry.

When it comes to spirituality, we deal with this situation quite often. We know we want to "be spiritual," but we don't really know what that means. We dabble in what we think is desired, based on what we see around us. Instead of borrowing a shirt, as in the story above, we borrow someone else's spiritual norm.

It's part of the human condition to want happiness, and we have all heard that a spiritual path can lead us there. But trying on different spiritual paths without making direct contact with our own souls inevitably leads to a dead end. The whole point of walking a genuine spiritual path is to dissolve all the illusions we carry so we can see into the truth of our nature. It is no good to trade one set of illusions—our habitual ones—for another, differently packaged set, however spiritual they may be.

Wearing someone else's shirt only distracts us from the internal work required to progress on our evolutionary path. Instead of discovering true and lasting happiness, we apply the latest technique or follow the hottest teacher—all to try to "fix" our anxiety. We may give up one norm from childhood, only to find ourselves living another one with a different lingo and costumes—however politically correct or socially encouraged it may be.

THE PROBLEMS WITH TODAY'S NEW AGE SPIRITUALITY

There is a huge wave of spirituality in the world today. Seekers want to move beyond religion and find solace in something different, modern, and practical. They think if they can be "spiritual but not religious," they will avoid all the pitfalls of organized religion, like guilt, abuse of power, and the degradation of women, children, same-sex couples, or even—through beliefs about humanity's right to control the world—the environment.

While I'm happy to see that more and more people are inclined toward spirituality, this new wave is not without problems of its own. I see plenty of spiritual aspirants who leave the religions of their parents only to substitute one dogma for another. Instead of being told that premarital sex is a sin, followers are told that eating sugar or not recycling is a sin. Again, we are missing the points of a spiritual path: truth, love, freedom, and real happiness. When we are seeking, we become vulnerable to a cult mentality, in which no one questions what they are told. And they act just as blindly, without consideration of how mandates fit their own conscience and values. In the absence of true, authentic spiritual guidance, through this blind adherence, we perpetuate suffering in ourselves and in the world around us.

Chanting Sanskrit mantras, cursing freely, getting symbolic tattoos, and becoming vegan are not real signs of a new age "I am rebellious" spirituality. Yet this is what most new age spiritualists do. This new age, "spiritual but not religious" wave has consequently developed its own types of spiritual norms. And these new age norms have become cults of their own. They offer shirts we think we must wear to enjoy the party and to be accepted or even appreciated, because everyone is either "with us" or "against us."

Here's an example: Vegans seem to love bashing meat eaters. I've been a vegetarian since birth. I've never tried egg or fish. And since 2002, I haven't had dairy products either. But I don't like labeling myself "vegan." These kinds of labels can create quite an ego force in our minds. I decided to disown these labels after seeing so many seekers around me beating the drum about compassion toward animals, without showing that same compassion to their fellow human beings. If we aren't capable of accepting our fellow human beings, then we certainly don't deserve to claim to be saving the lives of animals. Vegan culture is meant to protect animals, but it has ended up boosting the ego because people start to feel important and feel their lifestyle choice makes them better than others, which is doing the worst damage.

UNCENSORED SPIRITUALITY

Break the Norms offers a system of self-realization that is free from all pre-tentions and dogmas—all the wannabe spirituality. Instead of trying to "be spiritual," it's an invitation to just be *ourselves.* We don't need to personify an image of a perfect being. We don't need to attach a label to our sacred, inner lives. We don't need to ignore our doubts or fear that we might be asking forbidden questions. We can be uncensored.

Uncensored spirituality means that we inquire into subjects that tra-ditional religions or new age teachers shy away from. No question is off limits. We can follow our own curiosity. Whatever experience we have is exactly what we need to compose a question. There is no reason to exclude anyone, because it is about our relationship with ourselves. And we certainly don't need to force ourselves into someone else's spiritual "shirt" to experience the benefits of knowing our own nature.

Cults can stay in power only when the people who hold authority try to censor our deepest experience. Whether that cult is a traditional religion or a new age organization, controlling the spirituality of group members does nothing but keep power in the hands of a select few. But when we take the power into our own hands by looking into what is *true,* we will not get stuck in the spiritual traps that keep us from knowing our deepest essence. We can be free.

The norms in this chapter focus on common misconceptions our culture carries surrounding spirituality itself. If these norms stay in charge, we might avoid pursuing any spiritual path. If we think we need to wear a particular "shirt" in order to be spiritual, we may conclude that spirituality is not for us. But when we can be uncensored, we can discover what spirituality means for us.

NORM 1

TO BE SPIRITUAL,
WE MUST BEHAVE IN
A "SPIRITUAL" WAY

In January 2006, I had guests stay over at my tiny apartment in Flushing, New York. After dinner, I took out a popular Bollywood movie to show everyone.

"It's not an original DVD?" my guest exclaimed, as though she had never seen a bootleg copy of something before.

"No, it's not original," I told her. "Here, the original DVD costs nearly $25, while in India it costs only $5. Movie stores here get the DVDs directly from India and make copies. It's almost impossible to get original DVDs of Indian movies around here."

"Of course! I know that," she said. "But I am just surprised that Guru Ji [my father] would allow you to watch a bootleg movie. I mean, is it allowed? You should ask him. It may be a sin for a Guru or his son to watch the pirated version of a movie!"

I smiled, but she was not joking. She had deep concerns that my spiritual path was being tarnished by a bootleg DVD. She wasn't the first person I've met who had such a misconstrued definition of purity in spirituality. The human mind is obsessed with moral codes. We cling to anything that promises to make the world more understandable, more black and white. This is how religion and many leaders have swayed their followers. But the idea that God is judgmental is a man-made concept.

We are infatuated with the idea of adding some purity to our lives. We are told that we are sinners and, thus, we should "un-sin" our acts. A visit to Holy Ganges in India shows a crowd who wants to wash away its sins. A visit to the Pope or any religious leader shows there are many people who depend on such leaders to assure them that God will not punish them on judgment day. Many Gurus and religions attain their power by dividing the world into pure and impure. Their businesses run on promises to make followers more pure than they could become on their own. This practice may sell tickets and bring in funds to run their mission, but does it hold any meaning? We will get to this question and more in upcoming pages.

When I was in business school in New York I ran a *Positive Thinking* column for almost two years. As a spiritual columnist, I started receiving many emails and queries from students (and a few professors) who were seeking a spiritual solution to their problems. The majority of students who came forward to seek help also had many preconceived notions about what spirituality is.

As students in business school, their knowledge of spirituality was based on what they saw online or on various social media platforms. They all expected a philosophy major with a long beard and wrinkles around his eyes to get them enlightenment. But I was an Indian immigrant wearing jeans and hoodies with an iPod tucked in my pocket. Most of my fellow college friends and professors were exposed to a clichéd form of spirituality that emerged from the modern, more commercialized yoga scene. They saw trends like celebrity-endorsed veganism, chakra cleansing, and other elements that were packaged and sold as weekend workshops. They admitted that spirituality looked mystic and "weird" in their minds. Many of them later confessed to me that they were originally hesitant to ask for help because they weren't sure what I would suggest they do. They feared that I would be ardent about their adopting rules of behavior and conduct.

I struggled a bit in the beginning when I started giving them advice on managing life. This wasn't a role that I was expecting to take in a business school in New York City. The process became easy when I started connecting with them by sharing my story and encouraging them to share their tales. Soon it became a seamless process. The more they saw me in person and spoke to me, the more their doubts about a spiritual lifestyle melted away. The openness and warmth of my father helped me immensely in my journey. I knew the same method would work when I needed to connect with my fellow students and professors, too.

This didn't stop after college. As I moved forward on my journey to become a full-time spiritual advisor, I came across (and *still* come across) many people who avoid entering a spiritual path because they're afraid it is too mystic and may demand too rigid a change in their lifestyle.

ASSUMPTIONS THAT KEEP US FROM STARTING A SPIRITUAL PATH

Assumptions about what spirituality is supposed to look like can get in our way. Some of the most common obstructing beliefs that I hear are:

- I have to give up being ambitious. Making money isn't spiritual, I know!
- I have to abstain from getting married or having sex.
- I have to be vegan and eat an all-organic diet.
- It's just not for me! I can't meditate. I tried, and it just doesn't work for me!
- I have to identify as something, whether Hindu, Buddhist, or Christian.
- I have to dress up in a certain way. I have to wear conservative clothes or beads.
- If I dress a certain way, or own the right things, that will make me spiritual enough.

The list is endless. Such assumptions arise because of the spiritual circus going on out there. Mistaken beliefs, misinformation, and charlatans abound in the new age circuit. We can get lost in the conflicting dogmas, prescriptions, and techniques. There are websites catering to spiritual clothing. I recently saw a Kundalini Barbie in L.A. and shook my head. Spirituality is an industry now—and quite a flourishing one. The purpose of the spirituality industry was to inspire more connection, and now it is creating a division in an already much-divided world. There are the people who "look spiritual" and there are people who do not. The materialism is just another way to make people feel like they don't fit in.

The problem with thinking we need to be, look, and behave in certain ways in order to "be spiritual" is that we miss the opportunity to truly live a spiritual life. A spiritual life is a life of simplicity. It is not decorated with any accessories. Whatever I have read about Buddha, Mohammed Prophet, Guru Nanak Dev, Jesus Christ, and such godly giants, they all lived a simple life. There was no drama. I mean, I cannot imagine Jesus sulking over the number of followers that another spiritual teacher in his village had. Or Buddha hugging everyone in his discourses and throwing a fit when he didn't get his latte on time. Many spiritual Gurus can be seen throwing a tantrum when they are not on stage (and sometimes when they are on stage).

I can vouch that my father is a genuinely simple guy. His humbleness often moves me. The trick is in not *trying* to be humble. Simply be receptive to higher energy and grace. Spirituality asks you to just be. A spiritual lifestyle is not a status-friendly environment. It is comprised of compassion for others and ourselves—above how anyone may appear. The good news is that it is easy for us to be simple and, thus, become spiritual.

The most important benefit of such a spiritual lifestyle is coming to acknowledge our inherent worth that does not depend on external circumstances. We no longer waste time directionless, blindly seeking status or superficial belonging. We wake up with an intention to live a life of our highest potential. The temptations of materialism no longer distract us. We are guided by love and fearless energy.

BREAKTHROUGH
YOU DON'T HAVE TO BE A CERTAIN WAY— JUST BE YOU!

Real spirituality doesn't involve all of the hype and "shoulds" that surround the fake spirituality. It is not about being "cool" or appearing "holy." It is simple and effortless. It doesn't need you to be any way other than how you are. When you are being fully yourself, you will start becoming spiritual.

One of the most important invitations of our lives is the call to authenticity. When we tell the truth, both to ourselves and to those around us, it is a direct line to the divine. We are born as honest beings. If you don't believe me, ask a baby how your face looks. If they scream "potato," don't be mad. If they call you a princess, don't be too flattered. The opinion of babies keeps changing as they speak in the moment. Whatever they feel to be true at that moment, they say. We have inherited this authenticity in our souls. When we start to be authentic, we start to get back in touch with our source, the universe, God, or the divine self.

I'm not saying that lifestyle suggestions are not helpful—they have their place. But if the prescriptions become the aim instead of the means, we will be caught in a trap that distracts us from what we are really longing for. All suggestions should be just that—*suggestions*. A quality spiritual teaching does nothing but point us to what we already know deep down. It should help us become more *ourselves*.

CHOOSING A SPIRITUAL PATH THAT'S RIGHT FOR YOU

Do you like gardening? Do you live around nature, surrounded by forests or lush landscaping? Or do you live in the desert, where the land craves drops of rain? The only reason I am being nosy about your location is because I want you to look around. Look at the giant tree that sprouted from a tiny seed. A seed is a storehouse of massive potential. If it gets the right nurturing and the right environment, it can transform itself into something astoundingly beautiful. You and I are seeds with potential, too. We carry in ourselves possibilities that can lead us to the all-encompassing joy of divine light. And with the right nurturing guidance, we can transform ourselves for the better.

When we discover the right form of spiritual nourishment for our unique souls, we will feel it. We will relax and know that all of our quirks, talents, intentions, and longings are welcome. We will also know that our anger, fear, problematic desires, boredom, and weaknesses are welcome. We won't feel the need to dabble in the spiritual marketplace anymore. We can go home. And when I say "home," I mean the seat of our souls within.

Don't expect your life to magically be free of pain when you embark on a path of awakening. There's no way out of pain if you are a human. If you are looking for signs of relief to indicate that you are in the right place, you will always be disappointed. In fact, spiritual work often turns up the intensity of life. It brings habits and destructive tendencies to the surface so they can be met and integrated. But a good spiritual teaching will guide you to your strength, resilience, and unconditional wonder at the miracle of life. As a result, we get better equipped to handle pain when it arises.

As you uncover your true nature, it may be authentic for you to leave a relationship, a job, or simply wake up each morning and meditate instead of reading a news app. Because when you are on a true path, those choices will come from a deeper place. They will not come from some list of rules. You will feel moved to improve your life from inside yourself. That's how you'll know that what you are doing spiritually is working.

ADDRESSING MISCONCEPTIONS THAT KEEP US FROM LIVING A SPIRITUAL LIFE

Let's address four of the common assumptions I mentioned earlier, which can all function as excuses to avoid a spiritual path.

I have to give up being ambitious. Making money isn't spiritual.

When you are spiritual, you are beginning your journey toward becoming a complete and successful being. On this spiritual path, you get closer to having a good balance of financial success and spiritual intelligence. Your financial success will help you to become a better seeker, as you are no more consumed by worries of paying the bills.

I have often struggled with students who relate spirituality to a renounced lifestyle. They look at money as some sort of evil causing hindrance in their journey. Money is not evil. It is how we look at the money. If you are spiritual but are still struggling financially, then there is something wrong. You may be following a spiritual teaching that preaches material renunciation, which doesn't make sense for modern life. I spend a lot of my time in L.A., New York, Amsterdam, New Delhi, and various other big cities. If everyone in these cities gave up work and chanted mantras all day, they would die of hunger and pain. The modern lifestyle requires a solid balance of spirituality and worldly success.

Likewise, if you are consumed by money, you may need to focus on letting go of your attachment to material things and cultivate a deeper understanding with higher elements of our existence. Money can fulfill our needs, but if we start to revolve our lives around it, then there is no end to pain and misery. The spiritual path can help you make money and help you be happy while you're making it, too, instead of facing a daily drudge in which you exchange dreary labor and precious time for money. That's because the spiritual path helps us live our potential—whatever that means for us. It also infuses everything we do with more energy, enthusiasm, and clarity. And it keeps our attention on happiness that is unconditional, regardless of the state of our jobs or the financial fluctuations of our lives.

Of course, there will be stages on a spiritual journey when you may want to renounce everything. That includes relationships, money matters, and other worldly things, but that is not mandatory. It's your personal call if you wish to do that. But I always say that while it is easy to run to the mountains and claim that you have renounced everything, it takes a bold soul to remain in the world and maintain a balance.

I have to abstain from getting married or having sex.

There are certain sects of monks and spiritual masters who decide not to get married, but that doesn't mean that you can't get married if you want to become spiritual. My grandfather's brother (who was my father's Guru) also stayed unmarried because he felt like it. He did not want to involve himself with family and preferred to focus his undivided attention on spiritual attainment. But his brother (my grandpa) got married and had three children. One of those children became a renowned spiritual healer, got married, and had me.

Certain monks renounce sex because they feel it is their calling. It's a personal call to get married, to have sex, and to start a family. And you can certainly be married or sexually active and still pursue a sacred path. I come across various sects of spiritual masters who are comfortable leading a married life and yet are highly spiritual. They have a term for it: *Grihstha Asharam,* which means "my home is my shrine." One accepts a spouse and children as a source of strength on this journey. A hugely renowned monk, Shree Ramakrishna Paramhansa, was a married man, and he truly tops my list of the revered Gurus that I wish I could meet. He remained married and pursued a family lifestyle while changing the lives of countless seekers. Such spiritual followers renounce sexual misconduct and instead intend their sex lives to be beneficial to others and to their own attainment. I talk about this in depth in the chapter on sexuality.

Certain paths are more supportive of relational life (like Tantra) and other paths are more encouraging of renunciation and simplicity (like Zen Buddhism). The trick is finding the path that nourishes you to become more and more of what's authentic for you.

I have to be vegan and eat all organic food.

You are what you eat. This is the principal of Ayurveda, the traditional Indian system of medicine. Ayurveda states that you can heal yourself with a balanced diet, herbal treatments, and meditative practices. A significant part of Ayurveda is the belief that the mind heals the body in numerous ways.

The spiritual lifestyle does tend to adopt a similar practice of healing the mind, body, and soul together. When we consume foods that are difficult to digest, like a triple cheeseburger with chili fries, it is more difficult to enter the deeper stages of meditation.

As I mentioned earlier, I have been a vegetarian since birth, but a sage once warned me that the food I was consuming was preventing me from gaining higher spiritual experiences. He was referring to my fondness for fried food and soda.

Veganism and organic food choices are just more ways to have a conscious eating experience. It is good to be vegan because it will help you have a deeper meditation experience. What you take into your body adds to your meditative journey. Some spiritual paths, such as *Vaishnav,* recommend not using garlic and onion because they add aggressive energy to the body, causing a disruptive meditation. When I eat fried food, my meditation experience is different. In other words, I don't enjoy it as much as I do after a salad or fruit. Hence, I do suggest you to pay attention to food when you set out on this path.

I was born in India and am therefore a spoiled vegan. There are hundreds of delicious and super-healthy recipes in the Indian vegan system that you might find exotic to your taste buds. The vegan food that I have seen in the Western world is a lot different, and that's probably why some vegans end up being unhealthy. If you choose to be vegan, stay informed and do your research. In Indian vegetarian cuisine, there are lots of proteins and other ingredients for you to stay mindful and healthy. But treating nonvegans or people who eat mass-produced vegetables like criminals isn't right. There are monks who still eat meat and eggs and drink milk, because that's the kind of environment they live in. Being vegan doesn't guarantee enlightenment. I have never asked any of my clients to become vegan or vegetarian.

With a daily meditation practice, food habits often start to change on their own. Meditation brings you to a realization that all of us are part of this oneness. When we feel—not just believe—this oneness with every living being, we might prefer not to kill any animal just for our taste buds.

I have to be Hindu, Buddhist, Christian, or another faith.

Here's how I always answer this misconception: "You don't have to be an adherent to traditional religion. You just have to undo." The key to becoming spiritual is unlearning and dropping all our prior conditioning. Converting to a different religion isn't the solution. You can settle down into an ashram or even go on a journey to the Himalayas, but it won't solve your problems. Wherever you go, you take your baggage with you. Until you throw that baggage away, the misery will remain.

The label of religion is so strongly tattooed on our culture that one feels an orphan without having a religion. In many cultures, religion is one of the strongest signatures that a person carries. It is this sense of belonging to a higher power that makes religion so appealing to us. Knowing that someone is there to forgive our sins and take our worries away is a relieving thought. Certain people who crave more structure and ritual can thrive by sticking to a specific tradition. And others who feel stifled or controlled in a tradition will more naturally seek to let go of any religious identification.

I maintain that religion was not created with a wrong intention. I like to believe that religion was created to teach the art of living a contented life, which most of the new age movements promise to do. These religions were also probably the new age movements of their time, too. Over the years, they became organized religious bodies. Coming from the Hindu religion, I can attest that it is a refined religion that helps people to live a happier life. My limited knowledge about Buddhism, Sikhism, and Islam conveys the same message to me. The religion is not completely at fault. But it is the caretakers of these religions who decided to go on a power trip, making it a crazy ride for others. So it's important to always stay aware of *why* you are showing up to a particular spiritual or religious path—and to notice if you are receiving the help you seek. Is your spiritual activity helping you to be happier, more compassionate, more relaxed and energized? Or is it weighing you down?

There can be great benefit in committing to a lineage, if it helps you to be authentic and self-aware. I come from a respected lineage of Gurus in India. This lineage gave me the courage to leave the glamour of Wall Street and follow a spiritual path instead. I often think my choices could have gone completely wrong if my lineage weren't a noble one. I could have easily inherited the common beliefs of that industry, like greed, and carried on without any iota of guilt. Thankfully, that didn't happen. I'm so grateful!

Being in the amazing lineage of my Gurus not only exposed me to so many faiths and religions, but also prepared me on a practical level. But this was my personal experience. In my opinion, an authentic lineage or religion remains authentic as long as the leader of the lineage is authentic and physically active. Once the leader doesn't exist physically, followers will start to interpret the teachings in multiple ways and initiate a mess that's tough to clean up. That's what has happened to so many lineages and religions. A religion loses its authenticity the moment a real Guru is gone. Someone has to lead the masses.

I don't want to give you my answer of which religion you should opt for. Nor do I suggest that you carry on with the same religion as your family. That's because choosing a religion is not the solution. You can opt for the most peaceful religion in the world and still be a jerk. Or join with a fraudulent spiritual Guru and still remain honest. Instead of focusing on being in a religion or not, choose to follow your inner voice. Breaking the norms of rigid mindset will help you see the divine without the grip of any religion.

JUST BE YOU

Society feeds your ego and makes you do things that only benefit the agendas of society. Our society functions best when some people are made to feel powerful and others are made to feel weak. This power play keeps capitalism profitable. But when you become spiritual, you release yourself from the shackles of this type of conditioning. Once you land on a spiritual path that is right for you, or even while you are exploring what path is best for you, you need to go back to your roots. You need to get in touch with your reality because it's in your roots that all solutions reside. You don't need to chase the light anywhere else.

Once your misconceptions about spirituality start to disappear, you are left naked with only the real stuff. There are no tattoos, beads, yoga pants, or bracelets to display you in a spiritual light. You will be without reliance on any accessories and will look at life through a clear lens. You will be your authentic self.

With the right ingredients, the seed of consciousness will help you grow beautifully. There may be complications along the way, but they are all taken care of with time and insight. Being spiritual will attract authentic people and better circumstances in your life. You will get cosmic assistance when your vibrations start to shift to a higher frequency. All of these benefits appear when you are simply being who you are.

EXERCISE **UNCOVER YOUR AUTHENTICITY**

Look at yourself in the mirror. What do you wear that makes you feel like a spiritual seeker? Is it a Buddha T-shirt? Fancy beads? Bracelets? Some other accessory that's trending on Twitter? Whatever your spiritual accessories are, give them a break for at least a month. Don't share any spiritual quotes on social media or talk about how spiritual you are. Invest all of your energy in practical spirituality, like meditating twice a day or practicing forgiveness.

I also suggest mingling with people who challenged your emotions at a certain point in life. Meet them and see what's going on in your mind. Those who trigger discomfort in us can help us get to a deeper level of self-understanding. They give us an opportunity to see our reactions more clearly. Then we can discover our true selves, which is deeper than those reactions.

NOЯM **2**
SPIRITUALITY IS TIME-CONSUMING

As a culture, we are so stuck in our belief that if a treatment or process doesn't seem to bring quick results, we should avoid it. Plus, people tend to think that cultivating spirituality will dominate the hours in our days. This belief can prevent us from committing to a spiritual path.

When we look at the calendars in our phones, we are looking at the past or the future. We define time in the context of past and future as well. There always seems to be a race toward the future or a regret about the past. We often don't put any effort into experiencing the present. The truth is that when we are not connected in the present, everything will seem time-consuming.

We are also conditioned by our daily lives to do things only when they achieve a certain end, like completing a meal by doing the dishes or working to earn money. But in meditation, we are asked to "just be." At first, just being creates an uncomfortable feeling in the body because we've been trained to always be on the move, both physically and mentally. Isn't it unfortunate that there are so many struggles just to find the peace within us? Those struggles are all the result of thinking spiritual connection is some kind of goal that we need to "get" to.

This reminds me of a beautiful story about a man who was always on the go. He had read tons of scriptures and books, and he was known in society as a man with great intelligence. It was as if he wore an invisible crown on his head. But he didn't feel like any of his knowledge had helped him attain peace and happiness, so he decided to look for a Guru to help him embark on his genuine spiritual journey. He consulted tons of people, asking each of them where to find the most authentic Guru. Many people suggested a particular place, and finally, he reached the spot. There, he found a man sitting under a tree, singing songs and dancing to his own tunes.

"Hey, you!" the scholar said. "I need your help!"

"Ah, lovely you!" The man smiled and greeted the scholar as if he had known him for ages. "Tell me, my friend. How can I help you?"

The scholar felt a little uncomfortable with the man's overly nice gestures, but he asked where he could find a Guru. The man replied, "You will find him near a spot where the birds are chirping and the flowers are blooming. Lush green trees surround him. You will find him there, celebrating life. That's the man you are looking for!"

The scholar noted the man's advice and started walking away. After a few months on his tiring journey, the scholar reached a spot that looked very similar to what the man under the tree had described. The scholar was in tears; he felt as if he had found something very precious. He saw an older man who was smiling and looked lost in his own thoughts. The scholar rushed over to him.

"Wow! There you are," the scholar exclaimed. "I have been looking for you!"

The older man looked at the younger scholar and hugged him. "Take rest," he said. "We'll talk later."

"Have I seen you before?" the scholar asked. "You look familiar! Wait, are you the man I met a few months back? God, am I at the same spot I was at months ago?"

"Yes, my friend," the old man laughed. "You seem to recall it all now."

"Then why didn't you stop me before?" the teary-eyed scholar begged for an answer. "You should have informed me that I had reached you!"

"I did inform you," the man said. "I even described the exact location where you were standing. But you were too eager to chase something that was ahead of you in the future instead of simply finding it in the present moment. Your mind wasn't ready to find 'now' so easily. It wanted to add its own sense of timing and use all of the knowledge that it had consumed over the years."

BREAKTHROUGH
SPIRITUAL LIGHT CAN HIT YOU IN THE BLINK OF AN EYE

The reality is that spiritual truths are alive right now, in this moment. Our conditioned, habitual mind is what clouds our ability to experience the divine right now. It is also what tricks us into believing that we must engage some complex process to realize God—a process that will take years and years of acquiring new knowledge and techniques.

Meditation is the best way to cut through all of that bullshit. It helps us stop and look at what is right in front of us by shifting our attention from the chatter—from the cycles of reacting to what comes our way—to what is available in this moment.

In the present moment, there is no struggle with time. In meditation, there are no time cycles. Time is almost irrelevant in moments of deep meditation. Many seekers sometimes sit for hours and feel as if only a few minutes have passed by. And sometimes they sit for minutes and feel an eternity has passed.

It takes months to build a house, but it takes just a moment to enter it and start calling it home. So, why didn't we start living there before? Because the demolishing and the construction got in the way. Our inner homes are no different. We need to demolish what we have been trained to believe, so what is *real* can show itself.

In the same way, if we overconsume information about spiritual concepts, our minds will certainly tell us that we have to spend years acquiring more. I recommend that seekers avoid reading too much on topics such as Kundalini, chakra, meditation, mantra, and so on, and focus on practicing them instead. These meditative elements are more about experiencing than reading. If we try to conceptually understand all the information that is out there, we will never, ever get it all in this lifetime! If we stick to feeling and being in these sacred teachings, we will be able to shift our reality in a deeper way.

Spiritual information itself can trick us. It can simply add more layers of conditioning. For instance, maybe we read that an enlightened person sees blue light in meditation. And then we think that if we do not see a blue light, our meditation is not working. Our mind may say, "Maybe if I practice for ten more years, finally I will see a blue light."

Forget about the blue light! No spiritual effort is ever wasted. It is only our minds, telling us that we are far away from a goal that keeps us from recognizing that any color or type of spiritual light can hit us in the blink of an eye. Once we deal with our conditioned minds, the rest will be easy.

EXERCISE **EXPERIENCING TIMELESSNESS**

Write down the five things that instantly come to mind when you think about your past. Then, write down the five things that instantly come to mind when you think about your future. Observe all of these things carefully.

Now, write down all of the thoughts that are in your mind in the present moment. If they don't come, it's okay.

Shift yourself into a meditation posture. Take a few deep breaths.

Bring your awareness to your heart and slowly start chanting "Om." You can chant loudly or silently, but I recommend that you start with chanting slowly. As you advance in your practice, start with slow chanting and then do it faster and faster.

After a few repetitions of Om, bring to mind the thoughts from the past that you have written down. One by one, release each thought out into the universe. Trust that the universe will send these thoughts wherever they need to be.

Repeat the same process with the future thoughts.

Now, shift your awareness into the present. Return to deep breathing.

NORM 3

HUMANS ARE NOT WORTHY OF DIVINE LOVE

Love is the ultimate spiritual healer. A dose of love is infinitely better than any medication. When nothing else works, love works wonders. But when a human feels rejected by another human, they can seek solace in the divine, as divine grace is what keeps us going. But imagine if that door is closed, too.

Spiritual authoritarians can convince us that we are not worthy of divine love. They say that in order to be worthy of and accessible to divine love, we need to purify ourselves or adopt certain behaviors. And who holds the key to this purification and activity? These authoritarians, of course! Many traditional and modern teachers have done a great job convincing their students that they are the only way to reach divine grace. They say that humans can't get to God of their own accord and that we need the meditation techniques, yoga sequences, and processes they prescribe. These techniques can "fix" us.

I don't deny that many spiritual teachers go through a painstaking process to guide their seekers. But when those public leaders who are exploiting their seekers send out the message that humans are not worthy of divine love as they are, naturally and inherently, they do us all a great disservice. They perpetuate the belief that God is above the human race, and that our nature is separate from divinity. We learn that we are incomplete, and that something is wrong with us—even though we are just human beings. Therefore, we need a teacher on a high pedestal to give us what we could never find ourselves.

BЯEAKTHЯOUGH
HUMANS ARE WORTHY OF DIVINE LOVE

Rabindranath Tagore, who won the Nobel Prize in Literature, once said, "Every child comes with the message that God is not yet discouraged of man." The truth is that the divine loves. And love is the divine. We are born knowing this. While our minds learn to label, divide, and categorize love, the divine knows no divisions. There are no colors, castes, or religions on the divine's plate. The divine loves everything unconditionally, including you!

We need to fearlessly throw away the thought that the divine doesn't think we are worthy of its love. If we are breathing every day, if we are able to express gratitude every day, if we are able to hug someone and say, "I love you," then we are capable of being loved by the divine. Don't let anyone tell you otherwise.

I know this may sound too simple to be true. Or it may feel impossible for you to experience. The irony is that God's love is so simple, so close, that we don't need to go on a treasure hunt to find it. Instead, we should focus on noticing—and throwing away—any thoughts that say God's love is not with us.

If you are going through a challenging situation, don't blame God for it. The divine won't change your painful situations—because it wants *you* to change instead. There are messages and transformations waiting to unfold in you. What we call "pain" is actually healing in disguise. It is never proof that God does not love you.

There is no magical formula to realize that we are each deeply, profoundly loved. Some people can hear that message once and know it to be true in their hearts. Others need to hear it again and again. Still others need to experiment for themselves, and even to ask the divine for a sign of its love. Whatever we do, when we have the intention to know God's love, it will be revealed to us. So if you still have doubts about your worthiness, set the intention to realize that you are infinitely held and unconditionally supported.

This love is the foundation for all spiritual pursuits. If you have only one goal on your path, it should be to know that we are worthy of divine love, no matter what.

WHAT HAPPENS WHEN WE ACCEPT THAT WE ARE LOVED

Life transforms when we discover our inherent worthiness and when we realize the infinite love that's available to us. Here are some specific outcomes we can expect:

Acceptance

We will no longer feel neglected or outcast by God. We will feel accepted and acknowledged for who we are. This leads to uplifted awareness and a fearless attitude toward whatever task we undertake. Acceptance by the divine is the only acceptance we need.

Healing

When was the last time you experienced in-depth healing? We all have our share of scars and wounds. We love to hide our wounds, just like women who keep their jewelry locked in a safe, away from everyone's eyes. This suppression only intensifies the agony. Love is the ultimate cure for healing these wounds. In moments of meditation, let it all come out. Let all your pain and brokenness be felt by the invisible and unwavering stream of divine grace coming your way. You can't predict what the healing will look like, but it will happen.

Guidance

Fear and negligence in our lives keep confidence low. When we are afraid or insecure we tend to function poorly and make wrong decisions. But when we know we are being guided, there is no doubt. Each step is taken as if the next one is already taken care of. Guidance comes to us in many ways. It could come through a teacher, a friend, a stranger, a book that you just happened to buy, or even in dreams. I have received guidance in dreams many times. There are many sources of guidance. It is our awareness that needs to open up. When we know we are loved, we can trust the guidance that comes to us—even if we don't fully understand it right away.

Liberation

Knowing that we are loved liberates us from playing small, from the fear that our actions don't matter. We can raise our heads and actively engage in things that we believe in. You will start to build up self-esteem—and not ego—as your consciousness evolves. Then you can be free to follow your truth and your purpose.

Hopefulness

It's hope that keeps us going during tough times. Where there is no hope, there is very little to live for. When we are in the divine's shelter, we are not only hopeful, but also confident. I go through moments during which I have no clue what will happen next, but the divine partnership I have with God brings me hope in abundance. Life has a different quality when we are hopeful for miracles.

Security

Not feeling loved creates insecurity like nothing else. Growing up among spiritual teachers, I've seen many people cry like babies after they've been hugged or assured of love. Their insecurity had made them struggle, and just being embraced—to the depths of their soul—took away their worries. The security provided by the divine is the most powerful security there is. It can give us the confidence to move a mountain. Most seekers that I work with are victims of insecurity that was planted by a family member or a significant other. With divine security, you have all you need; you will never need anyone else's approval. There are no incomplete lines in the divine world. Everything is perfectly formatted. We are hung up on a belief that we are broken—or just have a miserable case of some bad luck. As we move toward understanding that the universe is perfect in its wholeness, we feel assured that there is never going to be a lack in the grand scheme of the divine. And since we are a part of this grand scheme, we cannot ever be lacking in our souls. Only voices of insecurity make us feel that we are not worthy. But the wholeness that comes from the divine says you and everyone is worthy. We don't need anyone's approval. We realize that we are perfectly secure no matter what. You can be whole by meditating upon this wholeness.

EXERCISE **DISCOVER UNCONDITIONAL LOVE**

Early morning is the best time to complete this exercise. On a sheet of paper, write down one intention. Make sure this intention is practical and able to be accomplished in two to three months.

Keep the intention in your altar or somewhere safe.

Sit in silence. Relax. Be mindful of your breathing.

Bring your awareness to your heart and plant the intention that you have created.

Express to the divine that if you love unconditionally, this intention will manifest itself in a period of ninety days. (You can choose the specific number of days here as per the nature of your intention.)

Now, release the intention out into the universe with complete faith.

Repeat this every day for at least five to ten minutes.

GOD? 3

nitially I was unsure whether I should use the word *God* in this chapter because of its numerous interpretations. I thought about going the new age route and instead using the words *divine, universe, energy,* or *higher self.* But then I realized that I want my words to wake you up. If I use the safe and accepted terminology, then I am just reassuring you about all of the current trending versions of God. So I am using the word *God* throughout the chapter (and book) so that we understand it in its totality.

Another thing I wasn't sure about was which pronouns to use. *She* or *he* would bring gender norms into the picture. It would be unfair to limit God with our limited labels. Hence, I will stick to using *it* to refer to God. Many ancient masters in India have often used *it,* and I find that very apt.

This labeling of the spiritual force in the world is just one of the many problems with religion. Here's a conversation that brings up another. One day, I was having a casual chat with our Pandit Ji, a Sanskrit scholar who performs rituals during special occasions. (*Ji* is a respectful addition to a name that's commonly used in India.)

"Pandit Ji, the world is messed up," I said. "People don't seem to understand anything about God, yet they bow down daily in his name. I find it very disturbing."

"What to do, Chandresh Ji!" he said. "People can be ignorant. Understanding God is the most important purpose in life."

"Exactly! Just the other day I was having coffee with a friend. He is a well-known name in the African-American community, and I am fond of him, but I was struck when he told me that God is black. And then, just a few days later, a new (white) student joined our meditation center and claimed that God is white. How crazy!"

Pandit Ji responded to me calmly and confidently. "They are both confused people, Chandresh Ji!" he said. "God is brown and we know it. You know that India has thirty-three million gods, right? We can't be wrong!"

WHO IS GOD?

The above conversation illustrates a problem with religion. Each religion in the world comes with a set of beliefs about who God is, what God does, and what God says. Each one dictates how we should think, feel, and behave. Whichever teacher or scholar is in front of us claims to be "right." And these teachers heavily influence our understanding of God.

Anyone can create and sell any idea they want about God and encourage students to live their lives based on that concept. But doing so is a most dangerous approach. It breeds confusion, doubt, and conflict. Instead of listening to God for ourselves, we listen to teachers who claim to have the answers. If we don't like what they say, we flit from one teacher to another but never find what we seek.

Today more than ever, we are exposed to a deluge of different versions of God in the "religion market." The God that is "sold" nowadays is often nothing more than a psychological drug we use to escape from our miseries. We visit temples and churches because we hope it will bring us some peace. Living among the Gurus, I often come across angry seekers who are simply following the Gurus to get the job done. It is as if they are saying, "Give me my peace so I can go home." But many are still struggling inside. We still get angry in traffic, we still worry about bills, and we still struggle in relationships. The list goes on and on.

The problem is that when we attach our understanding of God to a teacher, religion, or belief system, we never have a direct experience of God. Our mind only understands what it knows; we don't understand the unknown to its core yet. We either believe things blindly or make sense of them through a definite set of facts and information presented to us by experts. While we may have a fleeting experience of peace when we listen to teachers, it is only an imitation.

THE PROBLEMS WITH RELIGION

Our idea of God has often been taken from religious scriptures and passed on to us, from generation to generation. When we are born, we are asked to practice the religion our family is already practicing. While our family may be doing this with the intention of setting us on the right path, a narrow understanding of it can do more harm than good. We will thus continue to worship the God who will punish us, reward us, and never appear in front of our eyes. When adults assign a religion to us in our formative years, our limitless consciousness is made limited. We do not follow our curiosity and seek to know God in a personal way; we do not seek direct answers to our questions. In this way, we may be spiritually crippled from day one by having a specific religion forced upon us.

Further, religions can lose their meaning over time. Parents pass their interpretations to the malleable minds of the young, and then those children pass their interpretations to their kids. As each generation takes the torch, religious understanding shifts according to the circumstances of that generation. Whatever truth is contained in a tradition can become muddied.

I'm not saying that religion is inherently wrong or bad. I find tremendous inspiration and illumination within my Hindu tradition. I'm saying that religion has been corrupted. Here's a story to explain what I mean:

My college psychology professor had our class conduct a little experiment. The professor whispered a secret statement into the ear of the student at the front of class, and then asked that student to whisper the same statement to the next student. Each student was then supposed to pass it on to the next student, and so on. The statement circulated through our entire class of one hundred students. The professor randomly picked a student to recite his original statement. What the student said aloud was completely different from what the professor had whispered to the first student.

Then the professor randomly picked a few other students to reveal the secret message. Only about five percent of the class knew the original statement, while the rest of us were passing along a misconstrued version of it. This "telephone" experiment exposed a common misstep of human behavior: The original message tends to lose its meaning as we continue to add our own layers to it. The resulting message is far away from the original.

Our interpretation of God has followed a similar path. The masters—Jesus, Buddha, Krishna, Mohammed, and so many others—have done a fabulous job creating a path to discover the ultimate truth. We can call it God or divinity. But all these masters made a daring attempt to expand our minds. I like to be optimistic and believe that religion was created with honest intentions to help people. Unfortunately, each of these religions becomes a mystical set of doctrines that holds little or no practical meaning for many people.

A GOD WITHOUT RELIGION MAY BE THE SOLUTION!

Endeavoring to meet God for ourselves, independent of any teacher or belief system, may be the surest way to find what we seek. Without direct, personal contact with God, we will always feel that something is missing. God will always be an external, glorified phenomenon to us. We will always be bowing down to some dude claiming to give us a glimpse of it. We must go beyond our conditioned physical self to get a glimpse into a deeper reality of our existence.

If I had my way, I would ask every family to have their children meditate upon a God of no religion. Then children could discover the presence of God for themselves.

You see, God reveals itself in uncountable ways. When a Muslim prays toward Mecca, God is there. When a New York City yogini practices her sun salutations, God is there. When a child sings hymns of praise, God is there. The religious practices are doorways, but what is found behind the door cannot be claimed by any organization. The invitation of this life is to uncover the ways in which God reveals itself to us—in a personal way.

Most religious canons or spiritual traditions contain four parts: stories found in scripture, images found in art, philosophy, and practices. Of these four components, practices are the most important in my view. That's because the practices provide a direct experience of God. Of course, you could have a spiritual experience without any tradition at all, but my point is that direct inquiry is the reason for all religious teaching. It's also what often gets lost. Teachers and stories can give us maps, but we must be the explorer for ourselves.

In the *Bhagavad Gita,* the holy scriptures of the Hindus, God is referred to as *Saarthi,* which means "captain" or "driver." It is purposely translated as "captain" so that the seeker understands that their life can be driven in partnership with the grand intelligence of the divine—if they allow it.

The tragedy occurs when we read the scripture but don't find out for ourselves if we can trust God as our partner. We don't have enough faith that God will be a good driver because we don't experiment for ourselves. We hear the religious story and believe for a moment, but then we forget. This cycle never ends. That's because the stories can distract us from what we are looking for. The scriptures are meant to help us, but we often miss what they are all pointing toward. In philosophy, we can become victim to being torn between many interpretations so that the real message often gets lost.

To trust God, we must see, hear, and feel it each day. Before we can do any of those things, we need to clear through the religious programming that clutters our vision and produces static in our ears. We need to separate God from what we have been taught so we can make contact with it for ourselves. In this chapter, I will expose three cultural norms that produce the biggest barriers to realizing the truth about God. When we blast through these obstacles, we will have the opportunity to meet God in an innocent way. That's when the adventure truly begins!

NOᴙM 4
BOTH BELIEVERS AND NONBELIEVERS BLINDLY ACCEPT

In the matter of God, the world can be easily divided into two groups: one that believes in the presence of God or a higher energy and one that doesn't. The believers have built organizations and communities, support their religions passionately, and take part in activities that promote God, but the nonbelievers share "expert" scientific research in their efforts to prove that God does not actually exist.

These two groups are popularly known as the faithful and the atheists, respectively, and their claims leave them on opposite sides of the playing field. They call each other ignorant fools and all sorts of other offensive terms. I always have fun watching their debates. (You can watch a few of them on YouTube.) The interesting part of these two groups' discussions is that while they are using a different set of words to describe their opinions, they both function on the basis of a belief system. While one group believes God exists and credits God for all the goodness and wrongdoing in the world, the other group *believes* just as much. Atheists believe God doesn't exist, and they avoid references to God in their lives. Both groups are traveling in the same boat and floating in the same mindset; they're just sitting on opposite sides of each other.

I have never seen a winner in these debates because there will never be a winner. Both groups believe, and a belief system does what it promises: it makes you believe in a system. This blind war of belief has put the world in a severe God crisis.

THE PROBLEM WITH BELIEVING

Beliefs have a tendency to be misunderstood. We read or hear something we are "supposed" to believe, but without an experience, the belief is simply hearsay. This story explains my point:

In India, it was considered a high honor for a school to be upgraded to an English school. Students were trained rigorously to perform in ways that would impress the English inspectors in order to gain certification.

In one classroom, a teacher had picked her finest students for this crucial moment of inspection.

One student, who was always at the top of the class, was picked ahead of time to answer the question, "Who created you?" The intention behind this question was to show that the students were well versed in philosophy and religion.

The chosen student had been trained to effortlessly raise his hand and enthusiastically reply, "God created me, teacher, and I am so thankful!"

The day of inspection arrived. The management and staff were all excited, yet trembling with nerves. Everything was going well until something unexpected happened. The top student who was chosen to answer the question about God fell ill and couldn't make it to school. No one realized that he wasn't there, and the teacher was gladly showing the authorities that the students excelled in all academic subjects. As planned, she asked the ultimate question: "Who created you?"

The teacher quickly scanned the room to find her chosen student. A bit nervous, she repeated the question loudly, "Who created you?"

The room was so silent you could hear a pin drop. No one answered again. It was getting a bit awkward, and the teacher was uncomfortable. Another good student detected his teacher's nervousness and decided to raise his hand.

The relieved teacher smiled. "Oh, yes, please go ahead!" she exclaimed.

The student calmly responded, "The student who was created by God is out sick today. He couldn't be here."

The student who spoke was taught what to believe by rote. And without having an experience to back it up, he got the information wrong. This is our story. We are given certain information about God and told to believe it. So our concepts about God are not rooted in anything substantial. They can be misinterpreted. They can give us a false sense of safety. They can even trick us into thinking we understand God without ever meeting God face to face.

If we keep believing or disbelieving in God, we will always live a shallow life full of struggles and fears. That's because living in states of belief and disbelief only masks our wounds. It does not transform our shadow attributes, like fear, greed, lust, and the like. We may have a momentary feeling of relief when we think about our beliefs. That's because the mind loves to be certain, to follow arguments that seem logical. And when the mind relaxes, the body can relax. This process can mimic real peace. We may think we are healed. But whatever sense of relief comes from the mind's certainty is only a sliver of the healing that truly knowing God can bring. Wouldn't you rather have the real thing?

BREAKTHROUGH
GOD IS BEYOND
BELIEF OR DISBELIEF

Knowing God involves our whole being. True healing requires unshakable confidence in the vast, divine presence inside and outside each one of us. This is the only cure for suffering there is. And no belief can give us this confidence.

God is a deep experience. It is not a thing to be proved, but a phenomenon to discover. To move beyond belief or disbelief, we must look for God without "knowing" anything. We must admit that we do not have the answers, no matter what we have been taught to believe. Only then can we be truly open.

Most people avoid this state of openness. When we are finally willing to let go of our beliefs, we are vulnerable. Our beliefs are illusions that seem to protect us from the unknown. Letting go of them can be scary. But it is the only way.

To be open, don't engage this journey with the belief that God exists—or that it doesn't. Start with the goal of finding it. If you never find God, it's okay. You haven't committed a sin by not being able to feel its presence. A fish is always in the water. If I create a religion that glorifies the water, and make water look like an inaccessible body, I can't blame the fish if it dies feeling that it was never able to understand anything about water. A spiritual seeker's dilemma isn't any less. The godliness is all around us. We are made to feel that we are just too dumb to understand or feel it. Make mindful attempts to immerse yourself in the presence around you. No need to chase any outcome. God could still come in through the window you left open. What invites God in is releasing beliefs on either side of the coin.

In my experience with students, if you are not able to find God, you will go through frustration and pain, but somehow this pain will be a blessing in disguise. It will remind you that you need to continue on the journey. Your thirst has not been quenched yet.

Don't settle for anything less than a direct experience of God. The best way I've found to access God is through meditation. Meditation leads us into the state of openness that is required. That's because in the process of relaxing our thoughts and creating the emptiness within, meditation cleanses the beliefs that have built up on the lens of our perception. With a clear lens, we can see God in each moment. More than anything else, daily meditation, which directs the awareness into the soul, brings us into direct contact with God. Meditation shows us that God is beyond belief or disbelief.

So nothing I tell you about God will do you any good! I don't want to add another belief to your list. Go meditate. And then come back and tell me what you have found.

Don't expect to get rid of your conditioned consciousness about finding God in just a few days. It is so deeply engrained in us that it will take a while before you start to have any deeper experiences. But if you meditate with a thirst to know God, it will reveal itself to you. Stick with it!

EXERCISE **MEDITATION TO HAVE
A DIRECT EXPERIENCE OF GOD**

This meditation invites you to move your awareness to each region of your body, and then let go of your body to discover God. It is aimed at helping you see that you are not your body, but you have a body. When you can surrender your body, you can bring your awareness to the pure state of God's presence.

Try to do the following meditation out in nature, in a silent space with few people around. Wear loose, minimal clothing to allow your skin to breathe. I recommend that this meditation be done under the direction of a qualified spiritual teacher, at least for the first few sessions.

Close your eyes and take a few deep breaths. Sit upright and relaxed with your palms open.

Bring your awareness to your legs. Feel a line of energy starting from your left leg and traveling to your right leg. If you don't feel this energy, imagine that you feel it. Imagining will give you the same benefits, and eventually you will likely feel the energy. Do this for two to three minutes.

Move your awareness into your pelvis. Bring forth a sense of liberation and release all of the suppression you are holding. Do this for two to three minutes.

Gently take the awareness to your navel. When you were in your mother's womb, you received all of your energy through the navel. Acknowledge the power of the navel and sense the emptiness in it. Dive into this emptiness. Do this for five minutes.

Move your awareness to your heart. Observe all of the emotions strolling through your heart. Don't judge any of them; just go through them all. Do this for two to three minutes.

Now, with a deeper sense of your physical self, gently detach yourself from your body. *You are not your body. You have a body.* Meditate upon this thought and surrender yourself to the infinite sky or to the natural scene around you. Let it take over your complete being. Let yourself become completely loose. Stay in this state until you feel like getting up. As you get up and start any physical activity, observe every body part. Be sensitive and grateful to how healthy your body is. Feeling your heartbeat is one great addition, too.

NOЯM 5
GOD HAS A SYSTEM OF PUNISHMENTS AND REWARDS

Hurricane Sandy hit New York in October 2012. I was in San Diego at the time, but my phone's inbox was quickly flooded with images of giant trees on top of our Long Island house. Our home was so damaged that we had to stay elsewhere for almost ten months before we were able to move back in. When I returned to New York, I kept hearing everyone say that we had been the victims of a "brutal act of God." At the New York center of Break the Norms, I ran into Maria, who is on our cleaning staff. I hadn't seen her in a while, so I asked her if things had settled down for her after the hurricane.

"Oh, yes, we are good," she answered. "But Big Papa is angry. He doesn't like us and now he is punishing us with hurricanes."

This was not the first time I had heard people blaming God for a disaster. When my sister passed away at the age of nineteen, many worshippers of God claimed it was unfair. Moments like these can shake your faith in God. I remained silent after my sister's death; I did not cry at her funeral. But after nearly a week, I remember going to the terrace and crying my heart out while blaming God. I felt that God had betrayed me. At that point, the cultural belief that God rewards and punishes us colored my grief process. Luckily, my meditation practice eventually helped me to see beyond that belief.

As a spiritual advisor, I am asked the following questions time and time again: Why does God allow so much misery? And why can it not get rid of things like corruption, war, and the endless diseases in this world?

In an effort to answer these big questions, humans throughout the ages have created arguments. These arguments, and the beliefs required to prove them, are handed down through generations—which is the main problem with these lines of logic. They are products of our unconscious programming from childhood. Our parents also grew up with their parents and teachers rewarding and punishing them.

When adults find it too tough to punish children, they bring a third party—God—into the picture. God is used to scare kids out of committing any wrongdoings. Kids, who are each generation's tomorrow, become part of the God-fearing crowd. They pass the same fear on to the next generation.

As I have encountered more and more people from various faiths, I have noticed that their ideas about God produce fear in their hearts. People seem to be more God fearing than God loving. Seekers continue to do things in order to avoid God's punishment and gain more rewards, just as they learned to do with their parents and teachers. Because they have internalized this system, they may have guilt, which makes them think they deserve to be punished. And many seekers are in an ignorant comfort zone. They blindly accept these systems.

Those who feel like they benefit from this circus are the righteous ones who keep encouraging its practice. But in fearing God, we keep it far away from our hearts. Why would we want to actually meet this harsh, punishing figure? There doesn't seem to be any reason to seek its presence. As I've said before, if we don't discover God, we will stay stuck in our suffering. To eradicate punishing beliefs about God from the world, we must rewire our entire consciousness. The whole structure has to be uprooted.

BREAKTHROUGH
GOD DOESN'T FOLLOW ANY PUNISHMENT OR REWARD SYSTEM, WE DO

God is not a person or an object that is worrying about what we do and don't do. It doesn't have a list of desires that we must satisfy. Our morality codes are man-made, in order to establish peace and harmony. I am not against these codes, but I am against the way that the writing of them is attributed to God.

Poverty, corruption, wars, and all of the other disturbing scenes in our world are the result of man. Why must we bring in God?

Consider the topic of global warming. Science has shown that climate change has come from burning fossil fuels. If we continue to use products and indulge in activities that increase global warming, we cannot blame God for the disasters that occur.

What else do you blame God for? Is it rape? Or a killing spree? Or a plane hijacking? Whatever the event, the only force behind the action is a disturbed human mind.

It is limiting to see God as a man in the clouds who controls everything, so we can blame him when things go awry. That's way too easy! Doing so allows us to relinquish our responsibility for our own behaviors. If we can just blame God, we never have to look at our own disturbed minds. Instead of blaming God, we are all much better off if we work with God to bring healing to the planet and ourselves.

We don't commit sins for which we deserve to be punished. When we make a mistake, we simply haven't made use of all of the wisdom available to us. When we seek to know God, we will realize that we create our own suffering and harm. There is no reason for God to punish us—we punish ourselves enough! What we need to do is accept our problematic behavior and meditate upon our strengths to transform it.

GOD IS THE SOLUTION, NOT THE PROBLEM

In the space of God's grace, we can move beyond a system of reward and punishment—whether it's a man in the clouds or our own minds keeping track of it all. Doing so allows us to see our flaws as places where we need to change, not as life sentences that prove we are "bad."

When we invite God to help us, an amazing thing happens: We become free from the guilt that the reward and punishment paradigm brings. Without all the guilt and shame, we can use our life force to do beneficial things instead, like volunteer for an environmental group, become skillful healers, teach our children compassion, or meditate more often. Our example will spread to those around us. Awareness of God is contagious.

God is an existence that flows (or at least intends to flow) through all of us. It is up to us to tap into it or ignore it. God can invite us to experience its presence, but ultimately it is up to us to choose God. This is not a moral dilemma, but a decision to answer the call to a better life. Although our behaviors will surely cause more problems without God, God certainly does not punish us.

EXERCISE ERADICATE BELIEFS
ABOUT REWARD AND PUNISHMENT

This exercise is meant to reveal your beliefs about reward and punishment—and invite God to clear them away. Try to approach this with a sense of humor, without seriousness. Let go of judgments and attachments to what any of it means. Look at life as just a drama, a game, a play.

In your journal, write down a list of anything and everything you feel guilty about.

Then, write down any thoughts that come up involving you being punished for the things on your list.

Now put the list down and take a comfortable meditation posture. Focus on your breathing. Set the intention that your meditation will cleanse any beliefs that are false.

Meditate for at least twenty minutes.

NORM 6

**GOD EXISTS
ONLY IN TEMPLES**

The religious agendas and the marketing of so-called spiritual leaders amuse me. Not only have they made God an inaccessible element for seekers, but they often preach that God lives far away, in exotic temples. And usually, these teachers can take you to such sacred sites—for a small fortune!

It is damaging to learn that God lives in holy places but is absent from our own homes, our own communities. Then, certainly, God can't exist within our own hearts already. That would be too easy, too close! We believe that we must drag our bodies from location to location "out there" in order to achieve something that is far from our daily lives.

BЯEAKTHЯOUGH
GOD IS EVERYWHERE, IN EVERYTHING

When a seeker asks me, "Where is God?" I ask them, "Where isn't God?" God isn't in the future or the past. It exists in this very moment. God is not a phenomenon to be searched for somewhere. It does not need to be found in rituals or someplace far away. It simply needs to be discovered within you.

Just as good health appears when disease is eliminated, God will appear when you start to peel off the layers of conditioning in your mind. Spiritual practices have an effect that is like polishing a crystal. When you make an effort to remove the grime that has accumulated in your awareness, your spiritual luster is revealed. You see that God is not separate from who you are, right now, no matter where you go.

And when we discover that God can be met within, we can't help but see the same divine energy in everyone and everything around us. When we look into someone's eyes, we see that God can be met in that person, too. Maybe you have heard the word *namaste*. It means "the light in me recognizes the light in you." We are all made of this light. What a poetic way to express how God is in each one of us!

And God is also much more than just our individual selves. God dwells in every atom of the universe. God can be found in a stunning sunset, in a piece of art, in our pets. It can also be found in hospitals, garbage dumps, and traffic—nothing exists that is not God. The invitation of a spiritual life is to practice recognizing that God is always *here*.

GOD IS WITHOUT BEGINNING OR END

God has always been here. It was never born, and it will never die. We may start to wonder where this God lives or where it comes from. The irony is that we worry so much about the origin of God while we are still struggling to fix our own existence. If we put a date or time to God's birth, we will have to put a date to its death, too. What is born always dies, right? There is no benefit to wrestling with such questions. So don't worry too much about how God got here. Instead, have the intention to discover God right here, in this moment.

Our minds will always find it tough to accept that God has always been here. The human mind wants to prove to itself that it understands everything. It is just not acceptable to our egos that something so grand and important hasn't been understood. Personally, I don't think there is any fun in decoding the mystery of God. It would be like explaining poetry word for word or explaining the joke in such detail that everyone knows exactly what it means. We can continue to do our little experiments, but God's existence will always be a mystery because we have given so much hype to such a simple and beautiful presence. This presence is truly all around and within us. It is beyond the scope of the human mind to define and decode God. God is a song to dance to, but we sometimes get too distracted to hear the music.

There's a story that has been associated with so many Eastern mystics that I am afraid to quote any of them. But here's the message: Once, a saint was sitting with his legs pointed out toward a temple. A priest passed by and asked him to cross his legs because it was insulting to point one's legs toward a temple, the home of God.

"Then show me a direction where God doesn't exist," the saint responded.

In another story, a poet was asked to stop drinking alcohol in a mosque because it was the home of God. The poet responded by asking the priest to take him to where God doesn't exist because there is no such place, moment, or being. Call it divine, energy, universe, consciousness, whatever. Changing the name will not change the experience. But don't take my word for it. See for yourself.

THE BENEFITS OF SACRED SITES

It's true that God is everything. But it would be too overwhelming to live in this vastness in every moment. How could we drive to work or speak to our friends if all we ever saw was one big light? Sometimes a small window is the best way to see the magnitude of the sky.

The same is true when it comes to discovering God for ourselves. A portal into the infinite helps us to recognize God in ways we can relate to. That is the reason sacred sites are often dedicated to a certain deity.

Temples, churches, and other sacred places were built so that people could come together to meditate on a particular holy form. The ancient temples in India were strategically built so that meditative and cosmic energies were multiplied to a new level. Even now, so many temples in India are designed to give you a kick-ass experience of godliness.

Each of us will be drawn to particular doorways to the divine, and it can be great fun to discover which windows open our direct experience of God most powerfully. Growing up, I often joined my father on his visits to various spiritual shrines and religious places. I took joy in meditating in temples and churches dedicated to Jesus, Krishna, and Guru Nanak Dev, as well as the mosque at Ajmer. Of all the gods, I felt the strongest affinity for the Hindu Goddess Kaali.

I started meditating upon Kaali more often. At one point, I was feeling disconnected from her presence, so I went to my teacher, Guru Ji, for guidance. I told him how difficult it was to meditate upon her.

"That's because you see yourself and her as two poles apart," he said. "Look at her as your mother or your closest friend. With your mother or friend, you can discuss anything easily. Don't expect to connect with her if you see her as an alien being."

Through the lens of a persona I could understand, I could grasp the limitlessness of Kaali. I could go to her temple, sit with her, ask her questions, and listen to her voice. Then I could see her presence in all beings. My visits to Kolkata's Kaali temple—a Kaali temple loaded with images of Kaali as a mother—made me feel closely connected with her. At the same time, I felt like a tiny speck of dust in this universe loaded with miracles of God. It's a paradox. We connect to a form, like a particular goddess, and that form leads us to what is formless. Temples dedicated to one form of God are potent doorways to direct experience of the infinite.

But the infinite is not attached to any holy site. It is infinite, after all! The only thing temples and churches do is point us to a presence that can be found in every moment, in every location. If we know this, we can reap benefits from visiting them. But never believe any so-called "spiritual teacher" who tells you that you must go to their ashram or make a pilgrimage to some exotic place in order to be happy.

DISCOVER YOUR OWN PORTAL

I use Tantra teachings to help seekers meet with the divine. Tantra invites seekers to contemplate myths and images for particular gods. Each myth reflects a different aspect of the universe. So focusing on one myth at a time helps us to understand a particular quality of the infinite in a digestible way. Visiting the temple of a Tantric god or goddess can be a highly effective way to open your perception into the fullness of the divine. But make sure not to take my word for it. Find your own doorway.

Even visiting a small town or village where the demands of modern life seem less than what you're used to can provide huge benefits. Sometimes leaving a big city is all we need to connect to the silence within. If you go to small villages, you will find people who easily meditate because their lives are not as overwhelmingly full of stimulation. My experience within villages in India, Switzerland, Sri Lanka, and even certain small towns in the United States has been profound.

Allowing God into your life is one of the most revolutionary changes you can make. Basically, every chapter in this book is saying the same thing—clear out the crap so God can come in and show you the way to bliss. If this is the only message you receive from your reading, you will have everything you need.

Before you get ready to discover God, ask yourself if you are ready to afford it. If you are struggling in your career, relationships, finances, and other such worldly matters, discovering God feels like a cruel joke. Break the Norms is about first taking care of such issues draining you in and out, and then creating a spiritual lifestyle plan for discovering the infinite within.

EXERCISE **OPEN YOURSELF TO GOD**

Here is a Break the Norms practice recommended to create more openness to discover God. Keep in mind that there is no sure way. All practice like this can do is create circumstances for opening ourselves up to the godliness and letting it happen. The mantras offered in this exercise are meaningful aids: *Aham Brahma-Asmi* means "the universe/divine resides in me" and *Namaha Shivaya* means "I surrender myself to higher consciousness. I am receptive to this infinite consciousness."

The best time for this practice is before sunrise or after midnight. Wear a light white cloth. Light a candle or *diya* with clarified butter (available at Indian stores).

Take deep breaths for a few moments. Visualize your physical body in stillness.

As you inhale, let the sound of *Aham Brahma-Asmi* pass through your entire body. As you exhale, feel the same thing. Repeat ten times.

Take your awareness to your Third Eye (the space between your eyebrows) and repeat the mantra *Namaha Shivaya* for at least ten to fifteen minutes.

Take the last few moments to open yourself up like a flower blooming itself.

STRAIGHT TALK ABOUT EGO

My uncle in India started his career selling clothes on the street and ended up owning a fashion brand that has more than sixteen hundred stores. I once asked him what he thought the reason was for his larger-than-life success.

"I put my nose to the side when I do business," he told me.

The "nose," in this case, is the ego. Ultimately, my uncle had to learn to sweep his ego's twisted motivations out of the way in order to access his deeper intuitions about how to handle his affairs.

He experienced ego every time he hit a new high with his business, thinking he knew it all and didn't need to listen to any words of advice from wise teachers. His ego told him, "I have reached this level of success; I am the smartest person I know." Although he felt important, he missed critical details that cost him time and money.

In hindsight, my uncle could see the difference between when he followed his soul and when he followed his ego. When he followed his ego, he created challenges that could have been avoided. Once he learned to keep his ego aside, he was able to focus on his conscious desire to succeed. He hit rough patches many times along the way, but learning to ignore the ego and instead pay attention to his soul's deeper calling kept him going.

WHAT IS EGO?

Before we get too far into our discussion, let's first define the term *ego*. The ego is a slippery topic in the spiritual world these days. I have heard lots of creative descriptions for it. The ego is a filter, or the voice of "me"—and as a result of listening to it, we edge God out. One of my favorite ways to think of the ego is as an acronym for *edging God out*. You can also think of ego as *edging Guru out*. (*Guru* means "teacher" in Sanskrit.) When we live from our egos, we are so full of ourselves that we can't learn our lessons. We think we know everything, and we don't allow life to be our teacher. For a more in-depth exploration of Gurus, see chapter 5.

Each of us has God within. But we also have a condition in our embodiment that focuses on forgetting this fact. The ego fixates on pride, self-importance, greed, regret, control, fear, doubt—all the habits that cause suffering. The suffering is rooted in one overarching mistake: forgetting God. And in forgetting God, we also forget our true selves.

When your ego is in charge, you don't follow your true path in life. That's because you are seeking something outside yourself. You may be seeking approval, status, or to fit into a prescription of how you "should" live. It is the ego that gets conditioned by culture, families, and religions. It makes us believe we are failures if we don't live up to external definitions of success.

Any time the ego is in control, we are not open. We are running an old recording in our minds that says some version of these two stories: "I am better than everyone else" or "I am terrible compared to everyone else."

I was invited to Rishikesh, India—the yoga capital of world—for a humungous spiritual event. I was one of the speakers, and I shared this honor with many other honorary spiritual teachers from India and around the world. On the first day, a calm-looking, graceful lady was on stage, singing compassionate songs of the divine. She sang about love, forgiveness, and cultivating compassion in life. The seekers watching her were moved, and I was moved seeing them.

While she was singing, volunteers quietly started setting up chairs for the event that was scheduled right after her performance. The performer asked them to stop. The volunteers—mostly young kids—promised they would be quiet. The performer was visibly upset, and a few more words were exchanged off the microphone before she started singing again. The kids stopped setting up the chairs but remained next to them, hoping for a chance to get their job done. A few minutes later, the woman on stage stopped singing. The seekers cheered.

"Ah, she will give us blessings now," said the attendee sitting next to me. It was his first visit to India, and he had come especially for the event. The young volunteers had gone on stage and were asking the singer for her forgiveness, but her gestures kept getting angrier. She walked off the stage in anger, and her crew followed. Many of the seekers still sat with crossed hands, hoping to seek her blessings, while the rest of us wondered what had just happened. I won't mention her spiritual name here, but it translates to "messenger of peace."

If I had to paint a picture of the ego, it would be of that performer, who, while singing sacred music, allowed ego to take over everything. Ego is blind and believes that it is the only thing that exists in the world. Ego is deaf and cannot hear anyone else's opinion. Ego has two tongues so it can continuously talk about itself. And of course, ego does not have a heart, only multiple sets of brains loaded with fancy theories and all of the knowledge from intelligent-looking books. Ego is an ugly sight, but its ugliness is well hidden beneath masks deeply engrained on its skin.

EGO, ANGER, AND DESIRE

The ego thrives on two basic human emotions: anger and desire. We experience anger when the ego's desires are unfulfilled. And all kinds of suffering ensues.

Here's a simple example: The ego tells you that you are the most successful person on your block. You deserve a luxury car!

You feel inflated and think, "Yes, I will look very successful in my new car."

But when you get to the store, you realize that you do not have enough money to afford the car you desire most. Now you feel angry that you can't have the car you want. Then you get angry with your boss for not paying you more money. Then you get angry with your parents for not sending you to better schools.

Your ego feels deflated and tells you that you are a failure, less successful than everyone in the store. In just a few hours, you have gone from grand to denigrated. You feel resentful and cranky.

If you are lucky, you will go home and meditate—and realize what a ridiculous trip your ego has taken you on! If left unchecked, anger, desire, and ego can rule our lives. They can steer the consciousness in any direction they want, whether it be suppressing a desire or screaming at someone. Think about how someone can marry the person of their dreams, and then later cheat on that same person—those actions find their sources in anger, desire, and ego. Nothing can kick us as hard as they do. They often play around with us, enjoying how we handle (or better yet, mishandle) them.

Our mismanagement of ego, anger, and desire makes them monsters in the process. We need a way to become more powerful than the fluctuations of the ego.

THE POSSIBILITY OF EGO MASTERY

Although seemingly negative, anger and desire are actually powerful energies that can be channeled properly, forming a bridge to reach your higher self. When we can see through our misguided beliefs, we can master the seemingly problematic aspects of our humanness. This awareness helps us to see clearly and make good decisions.

I want to make one thing clear: ego, desire, and anger are not your enemies. They are your friends who just need more guidance. Instead of letting them be the energy centers that govern your life, you need to reverse the role and be the one who governs *them* from now on.

The creator did not make a mistake in creating these emotions: Whatever we have in us is there in order to experience the life process. There is no accident in our evolution or creation. We are constantly told that our desires should be shunned, that anger is our enemy, and that ego is evil, but these elements also help us in many ways. If I didn't have a desire to share my message, I wouldn't be writing this book. If you weren't dissatisfied with or probably angry about the way things were going in your life, you wouldn't be willing to take a step to improve it (and read this book). If there was no desire to raise awareness, you wouldn't be taking the steps you're taking now.

There are many instances when anger, ego, and desire can motivate you to do something better, but these moments are hard to come by or easily missed. In order to start recognizing the hidden gifts of our humanness, to access our spontaneity, drive, and creativity, we must learn to master our ego. We can start by looking at the following two norms, and breaking through to the truth.

NORM 7
THE EGO IS EVIL AND
WE MUST DISPOSE OF IT

Obviously, no one strives to be a jerk. Well-meaning spiritual seekers often see the harm caused by their egos for the first time and want to change things. This is an honorable and essential moment on a spiritual path. While this awakening can lead to incredible spiritual progress, it can also be misconstrued as evidence that our human foibles make us "bad." In an effort to be "good," seekers deduce that they must purify themselves of their sins. They must renounce the entire ego.

Renouncing something can seem like a relatively easy task. We can run to the Himalayas and declare that we have renounced sex, desire, and ambition. But why must we physically relocate ourselves to do it? When we declare renunciation and move into some ashram, we bring along the baggage that caused us to move in the first place.

At ashrams, seekers often perform severe austerities. They may deprive themselves of food in an effort to renounce desire. They may practice rigorous asana for hours, trying to quiet the mind, and eliminate any anger or sexual urges. They think if they can achieve super-human pretzel shapes with their bodies, they will gain freedom from the grips of their egos.

While yoga can be a valuable tool if applied properly, it can also become a system of self-punishment. So can any spiritual practice.

Instead of offering hope, love, and growth, practices aimed at renouncing ego can fuel shame, self-loathing, and attempts at control.

When misguided, seekers are not renouncing their egos. They are trying to eliminate the fact of their humanness. They look gaunt, empty, and sad. They are trying to accomplish something that is not possible. That's no way to receive the blessing of a human life.

BREAKTHROUGH
EGO CANNOT BE THROWN AWAY—IT CAN ONLY BE MANAGED

No part of the ego is good. All of it is an obstacle to truth. But no matter how much damage it causes, the harsh truth is that we can neither run away from, nor suppress, our egos. Suppressing ego may seem simple and easy, but it's not a solution—because it's not possible! The ego is a fact of being human. If we try to repress the ego, all we do is invite more trouble as its forces go deeper underground and work in ever more subtle and invasive ways.

So instead of aiming to dispose of the ego, we must focus on what *is* possible: managing the ego. That means looking honestly at our suffering and learning to recognize when our egos have taken control of our attention. We can learn to see the ego's fixations, but not follow them. It's like dismantling a bomb before it detonates.

Sometimes it takes a big, self-inflicted disaster to occur before we can admit that the ego was calling the shots. You might have an affair and lose your partner. Only then do you admit that your anger got out of control, causing you to unconsciously look for revenge. But the good news is that you can learn to spot the sneaky ego before it does damage. That way, you can learn the lessons you need to learn without having to go through unnecessary suffering. Because if you refuse to learn, God will make sure you get the message, one way or another!

When we learn to manage the ego, we can instead learn to rely on a connection to our true selves, to God within, to handle ourselves and our world. This is the source of an incredible potential, which manifests into a blessed reality. We can only access divine help if our egos are out of the way, which opens doors to hidden messages and to fresh, new consciousness. Only with the ego in check can we have true love in our relationships (see chapter 6).

The process of learning to manage ego must be gradual and gentle. Do not torture or punish yourself! Instead, focus on cultivating the following three qualities: acceptance, presence, and humility. As problematic as humanness can be, it also includes incredible graces and talents. So by focusing on developing those, you will have much better results managing your ego.

Acceptance

The ego does not want you to accept yourself or others. It wants you to try to change or dominate things. That's its nature. Instead, I recommend that you begin a practice of learning to accept situations as they are. Don't try to steer them.

When you accept life, the ego has no choice but to sit down and be quiet. Only then can we go beyond the conditioned patterns of mind. If we remove our attention from our ego's strategies of control, we can remember God. God lives in each moment, underneath all the strategies.

And when you access God, you access real solutions. You can be moved from within, from an authentic place. Fresh, spontaneous inspiration can come through. And circumstances wrought with suffering often change of their own accord, without our having to "figure out" what to do.

The miracle is that acceptance allows you to be responsive instead of reactive. Reactions come from our ego conditioning. They do not have any reflection or awareness. Someone curses; you curse back. But a response is mindful. A response means you try to understand why other people are reacting in a certain way. It allows you to focus on the solution instead of just the problem.

Responses are also free from expectation. We expect a problem to escalate when we are reacting. But when we respond with acceptance of someone's flaws, we don't know how they will act. Spontaneity can happen.

Acceptance can start with family members, spouses, and friends whose actions don't align with our way of life. If you are adamantly vegan, a disciplined meditator, or live by any set of specific values, try to look at others' actions and choices with a new curiosity and accept their ways as you accept yours. If you find yourself in a conflict, pause and give yourself the space to respond without trying to control anything. Cultivating skills in this way will help you to keep your ego in check.

Presence

The ego gets its oxygen from the past and the future. The ego can dwell in the past—brooding, wishing things had been different. It can also project into the future, tricking us into believing that we will be happy in some future moment—as long as the circumstances look a certain way.

The problem with following the ego forward or backward is that we are never fully in reality. We are in the world of illusions: the illusion that we can control an outcome or that we should have behaved differently. Either way, when we resist reality, we struggle.

That's because we block out the divine intelligence that is there for us, guiding and sustaining us. Ego and creativity can never be together. If we are wondering about the outcome of our actions, we cannot act from an authentic, divinely inspired place. If we are trying to do something that will prove we are "the best," we will only be the worst at heart.

But when we ignore the ego and focus on the moment instead, our efficiency comes out. If we are present, the ego cannot sabotage our genius. We can act from a well of insight deep within. There is no fear. We can just be ourselves. We realize that we are full of light and bliss. This is the highest form of meditation.

This freedom is what we are really after, anyway. The conundrum is that when we try to control it, we actually block it.

You may be wondering, "How can I be present?" At any time, you can bring your awareness to your heart and ask yourself, "Where am I?" Sure, you may be physically present somewhere, but this question refers to your state of awareness, not your actual location. You will be surprised to find that most of the time, your awareness is in the past or the future. Simply asking yourself this question often acts as a great reminder for coming back to the present moment.

Humility

Do you feel special when people like, comment on, or retweet a picture of you doing yoga or meditating? It's okay to say yes. Social media has inspired many people to kick-start a fitness routine or give spirituality a try, but it has also increased our need to be liked. I recently read somewhere that if Facebook were to shut down for a year, people would walk down the street shouting, "Do you like me? Do you?!"

In India, we hide our meditation beads in a tiny bag. We put our hands in the bag and rotate the beads around our fingers while chanting a mantra. This practice symbolizes the desire to remain incognito on our spiritual path.

When we don't flaunt our spirituality, as the ego would have us do, we can be humble. Humility is the acknowledgment of who we really are. Everyone wants to be somebody important. But with humility, we can just be human. We can detach ourselves from the labels of society. There's no pressure. What a relief!

In the face of humility, the ego curls up in the corner like a puppy dog. Then, we can really start to *live*. We can live for ourselves instead of slaving away for the fancy house or trendy fashion items. Our bank account does not have the same power over us.

The irony is that we can only truly succeed when we are humble. The stress we place on ourselves by trying to be "someone" sabotages whatever intentions we hold. The kind of happiness you are really after comes only from following *your* bliss, not someone else's.

So practice humility. Start off by not always sharing your meditation or yoga experience on social media. Remain silent and try not to brag about your spiritual progress. Carry this out responsibly. Yes, sometimes sharing your experience may inspire others, but chances are, it makes you a self-proclaimed "enlightened soul," too. Be aware.

You can play with the quality of humility in another way: Practice being *nobody*. Every now and then, try to disappear into the crowd. You may have been taught to stand out in a crowd, but try breaking this norm often. Be nothing in the crowd. Be a stranger. Go to places where no one knows you. Let them talk to you as they please. Make friends with strangers.

Be gentle with yourself as you learn to master your ego. Pause often and enjoy the lightness that comes when you lay down the ego's endless load of demands. Celebrate each time you realize you did not react during a charged moment. And forgive yourself quickly when you miss something.

EXERCISE **WITNESS THE EGO**

A person who is dominated by a problematic ego is disconnected from their center. In this meditation, I request that you move into the center of your navel area. Be in a place where you don't feel judged. Create a sacred space for yourself where you aren't hunting for anything. The mantra in this exercise, *Neti Neti,* means "Not this, not this."

Sit silently for a couple of minutes. Breathe gently. Keep your palms open and your fingertips next to the navel for a few moments.

Keep your awareness on your navel and invite your thoughts in. Watch them without judgment or identification. Continue to do this for the next few moments.

Next, look within and ask, "How do I define myself?"

Pause for a moment and then ask, "Who am I?" Keep watching all of the answers that come your way.

Then begin to reject all the answers that come your way. The sages recommended using the mantra *Neti Neti* for all answers that come to you during such processes. Any answer that you receive will be from your mind, not from your inner self. After you reject all answers, your mind shall be devoid of all conditioned answers and then you can create space for reality.

Next, look into the things and people that you want to change or control. Witness the memories arising of your actions in those situations.

Release the need to be in control. In your mind's eye, picture yourself releasing the need to feel important all of the time. Picture yourself releasing the need to blame others.

Stand up. Stay alert to your awareness. Repeat all of the above steps, while standing, in a gentle manner.

After a few rotations of sitting and standing, sit back down and be in silence.

NORM 8
WE SHOULD ELIMINATE DESIRE

Once, I was in India and sitting in the audience at a *satsang* (*sat* means "truth" and *sang* means "company"). *Satsang* refers to engaging in the company of truth with like-minded seekers. The speaker was a woman dressed beautifully in orange. In India, monks dressed in orange are the ones who have renounced the material world and given up all of their desires. I had just finished my talk on the same stage and had decided to stay and listen to her. Her talk went over well with the crowd. Everyone had a "spiritual vibe" until one young guy raised his hand.

"You talked about renouncing desires and said that money, or desire for money, is evil," he said. "I am not able to understand this well! If you don't have a desire for money, you wouldn't have been able to create this event or build such huge spiritual centers in the first place. Can you talk more about that?"

The woman smiled and answered him, but he wasn't convinced. She kept saying that money was evil, and he kept asking why, then, he was being asked to donate so much money at the event. The conversation continued and ended up making the woman angry. She suppressed her anger by tightening her brows, smiling at the audience, and walking out. I was supposed to see her after her talk, but she canceled our meeting. The young man remained on the floor, the object of glares from other attendees.

I am not judging either person in this situation. The woman's Guru probably taught her that everything is *maya* (illusion). Many Gurus teach the belief that everything is *maya,* and because all objects of desire are nothing but an illusion anyway, one should not have any desires. The young man was confused by the concept that all desires are illusions, especially when this same woman had been encouraging people to donate and had built a beautiful spiritual center. It all starts from a desire, and nothing is wrong with that. The young seeker was just trying to make sense out of the profundity of the talks at the event. I have come across many seekers who are perplexed by the messages from spiritual Gurus.

This type of spiritual confusion happens everywhere. In 2012, dozens of billboards in Manhattan advertised that the world was coming to an end, listing a phone number to call. Upon calling that number, people on the other end of the line tried to convince you that, since the world was ending, you should let go of material desires and donate all of your money to them.

What are we supposed to do when spiritual messengers and religions are confusing their seekers? By telling people to give up on their desires, teachers are often planting an even bigger desire: the desire to be desire-less. I meet many clients who want to detach themselves from their desires and live like monks. But these same clients also want to be the most famous person in Hollywood or a wealthy Wall Street tycoon. We certainly cannot pursue fame and wealth if we have such rigid ideas about renouncing desires. There is a major contradiction that needs to be addressed.

Here's the thing: It's impossible to get rid of desire completely. Desires are tattooed in our consciousness. They are like shadows we can never get rid of. Anyone who has ever tried to become desire-less can attest to this fact.

If a teacher tells me that all desires are suffering and I need to eliminate desire to be happy, what happens? I go home and get hungry and feel bad about my desire to eat. It's a no-win situation. As long as I am trying to eliminate desire, I will always feel like a failure.

I'm not saying desires don't cause trouble. Of course they do! Unfulfilled desires can make us suffer. It's common to think that we will only be happy at some future time, when we have everything we want. If we don't get what we want, we may feel weak and inferior to those who appear to "have it all." Oftentimes, our unconscious desires are nothing but a product of what we see in the external world.

Unconscious desire can also be a problem when we *do* get what we want. As soon as one desire is fulfilled, we move on to the next desire. In today's world, it's rare to pause and simply be grateful for what we have. Fulfillment gets lost in the tangle of unconscious desires.

The problem is *unconscious* desire, not all desire. We simply don't know how to relate to our desires. We learn to see our lack of fulfillment as an obstacle to our happiness. And we learn that we should focus our attention on removing that obstacle by fulfilling the desire. In doing so, we overlook the contentment that we do have, in each moment.

Desires have become like compulsive disorders. We either obsess over what we want, or we obsess over how to stop desiring. We don't learn to discern which desires are worth following, and which desires are better off forgotten. We let our unconscious urges drive our chariots. Or we try to knock the driver completely off the seat, and wonder why we lack direction and fulfillment. It's crazy making! But with just a tiny attempt, we can begin the transformation from compulsive disorder to conscious order.

BЯEAKTHЯOUGH
CONSCIOUS DESIRING IS THE WAY TO GO

In order to cultivate conscious desires, you need to understand the true nature of desire. Not all desires are problematic. Desires can be profoundly generative. They can propel you forward in positive directions and point you toward your purpose in life.

The desire to heal your wounds is certainly useful. Often, this desire for wholeness is the first step on a lifelong path of spirituality. If you are reading this book, there is a desire in you to question your conditioning and learn how to change it.

The key to a fruitful relationship with our desires is consciousness. A conscious desire is free from all compulsion. It has no panic and no struggle. It comes from deep inside, not from the pressure of society. When our desires come from a place of comparing ourselves to the neighbors, or someone who we think has it all, we are placing unnecessary demands on ourselves. And these desires are a problem, whether or not they come to fruition. Conscious desires are never a problem because they reveal what is truly important in our souls.

When desires are conscious, we know which desires to follow and which desires to ignore. Instead of trying to suppress our desires, we seek to come face to face with them, without shame. The breakthrough comes when we realize that if we are conscious, we can *choose*.

That means we are free to set goals. We are free to go after what we want. We can have a Rolls Royce. We can have a hundred Rolls Royces. We just can't let them own us. We know the Rolls Royces are not what makes us happy. We know that our fulfillment would not leave if our cars were lost or stolen. And we know if we never have fancy cars, we can still be deeply and profoundly happy. Now that's freedom.

THE SOUL'S CALLING

A conscious desire reveals the soul's calling. It is the ultimate fuel to our dreams. Think of conscious desires as magic carpets. They take us toward our divine destination, infusing energy into every action.

When we meditate, we will know which desires are propelling us toward our purpose, and which ones are distracting us. We will see what happens when our egos mingle with an unconscious desire. Be suspicious if you notice yourself trying to force an outcome or compete with someone else. These crazy thoughts can be our greatest teachers. If we do not see them and learn from them, they will distract us from our path. Keep coming back to your own awareness. The desires that show the soul's calling rise to the surface, making us feel whole and holy. The ones that don't will fall away.

With a clear head, we will know where to invest our time and attention. We will move through the world with honesty and courage. This is the only way to find true success. Even if we manifest an outcome perfectly, it will only bring more suffering if it stemmed from an unconscious desire. True success has no hustle in it. It is peaceful. It is holy. It is our soul's calling.

That's what we are all longing for anyway—to follow our soul's truth. The outcomes don't even matter as much as we think they do. When you are in alignment with your soul's calling, it may look completely different than you thought it would. And it will certainly look different from your neighbors' callings! That's where the freedom to just be yourself comes in. It is better to follow your own bliss and make tons of mistakes than to follow someone else's bliss perfectly. And let me tell you, following your conscious desires is the best ticket to both inner and outer happiness.

DO NOT MEDITATE TO ESCAPE FROM YOUR DESIRES

Many seekers start meditating to escape from their desires, because they are taught that desire is the evil part of the spiritual journey. I want to make it clear that you should never meditate to run away from desires. You should meditate to go one-on-one with your desires.

Meditation can teach you to understand your desires and transcend them by achieving transparency. The Break the Norms meditations are Tantra-based, designed to get the seeker to meet their desires. No masks. No suppression. Just coming out from hiding. Doing this is like watching a mirror. We can understand ourselves on a one-on-one level. There is no more hide and seek. We realize that we cannot bypass the problems, that they will haunt us wherever we go.

Meditation can teach us to act upon our desires and attach meditation to them. This is the Break the Norms lifestyle.

EXERCISE **BECOME CONSCIOUS OF YOUR DESIRES**

This exercise is for someone who is meditating every day. If you do not meditate, all of these questions will be irrelevant. So first establish your meditation practice and then do this exercise. Revisit this exercise at least twice a year to see how things have evolved.

After your meditation, connect with your silence. Write down the answers to the following questions:

- What do I desire the most?
- Why do I desire it?
- Where does my desire come from?

- Does this desire fulfill me in a positive way?
- Is my desire out of necessity or out of happiness?
- Do I feel guilty about having this desire?

Ask any other questions that help you delve further into your desire.

You don't need to "do anything" with your answers. Simply allow your awareness to reveal its clarity to you. In the next few days or weeks, notice if you feel moved to take any actions.

Re-answer the same questions after three months. By the end of the year, go through your questions and see how much you have evolved in your response toward your desires.

TO GURU OR NOT TO GURU?
THAT IS THE QUESTION

Picture a baby on the day he is born. He is vulnerable, open, and ready to blossom. Now imagine the doctor does not show the baby to his mother yet because he feels that the baby is not ready. The baby is not aware that he has a mother because he is just a tiny infant. Now fast-forward to a few years later and the child has not yet been allowed to meet his mother. Someone determined he is still not ready to meet her. Another few years pass by, and the adult is angry and frustrated with life. He craves unconditional, motherly love. But again he is told that he is not yet ready to meet his mother! He is now an elderly adult and he is sick, taking the last breaths of his life. The adult confesses to his loved ones that he wishes he had met his mother. They tell him that they will pray it happens in his next lifetime. It was never that his mother wasn't alive and he wasn't able to see her—he was always "not ready yet."

This sad story illustrates what happens when we go through life without ever meeting God. We feel just as devastated and hopeless as a baby screaming for his mother who does not come. We never get to feel unconditional love. We do not bloom into the full person we are meant to be. Our life passes by, and we conclude that our presence on earth had no meaning, no joy, and no purpose.

In the same story, imagine if there is a person who not only makes the meeting of mother and child possible, but also lets the child understand how special her mother is and how sacred this relationship is!

Such is the role of a Guru. A Guru helps to remove the obstacles that hinder our meeting with the divine. Our religious belief, society, teachers, or our own conditioning set up such obstacles. An authentic Guru will clear the hurdles just the way morning sun clears away darkness so that a beautiful day can dawn.

THE EGO KEEPS GOD OUT

Remember our discussion of ego in the previous chapter? Well it's time to bring our trusty old friend back to the forefront of our conversation. The ego is like the doctor in the story above, always keeping love out.

We can also think of the unchecked ego as a bodyguard around our hearts. Stuffed full of judgments, fears, anger, projections, reactions, and conditioning, the ego builds a concrete wall around our hearts. This wall does its best to give us a feeling of security by keeping everything the same and not "rocking the boat." But the irony is that in protecting us from everything, it keeps out the only thing that gives us peace—unconditional love. The ego's voice is the bodyguard around this wall. It makes sure nothing—including love—gets in or out. The ego and all its voices are just doing their job: protecting the status quo.

In a moment of silence, we may feel a pure longing for unconditional love. But the ego walls harden and tighten. The voice of the bodyguard says, "No way are *you* getting in. Unconditional love would break down these walls and we would be left without protection." Our minds become full of doubts, excuses, and busyness, and we forget the moment of longing. We keep our heads down and keep moving along.

Each of us has a personal ego, as well as a collective "super-ego." While the personal ego focuses mainly on maintaining our individual status quo, the super-ego focuses on keeping the collective status quo. This is where we may encounter shame or guilt if we want to challenge what we've been told at a more global level, by religion, history, politics, and our families.

To understand the super-ego, it's useful to recall the metaphor of the doctor who won't let the baby see his mother. The baby's natural instinct is to reach for the unconditional love of his mother, but the doctor kept saying, "Not yet. You are not ready yet." Take out the word *doctor,* and replace it with *teacher, priest, rabbi, self-proclaimed Guru, yoga teacher,* or *self-help expert,* and you will understand how even spiritual work can continue to keep love out. We are told that we must say ten Hail Marys, stop eating meat, or follow ten steps before we can be pure enough to receive God. We get the message that our humanness, as it is, is not "good enough" yet to meet God.

So between the ego, which tries to protect our hearts from any "threat," and the super-ego, which makes darn sure we listen to the voices that come from outside ourselves, how can we break through to freedom and unconditional love? How can we stay guided and nurtured in this arduous journey? How do we get access to the secrets of a happy life and be showered with divine love? How do we experience the invisible phenomenon called God?

The answers to all of these questions are found in one word: Guru.

THE GURU LETS GOD IN

The word *Guru* is a combination of two words: *gu* and *ru. Gu* means darkness, and *ru* means the one who eliminates darkness. Hence, a Guru is the one who steers away the darkness. The darkness, in this sense, is anything that keeps us from knowing our true nature, from seeing God in each moment. It is what keeps unconditional love out. The darkness can also be understood as—you guessed it—the ego.

The darkness of the ego includes the cycles of addiction that we can't seem to control. It can be the moments we feel so alone that we can't stand being alive one more day. It also includes the squawking that goes on in our heads when we try to sit still and just be. It's this metaphoric darkness that clouds our lenses, which makes us believe that our lives don't matter, that happiness cannot be possible.

The Guru polishes our lenses, so we can see the truth clearly. The Guru lets God in. Basically, a Guru shows us the state of our egos, and invites us back to a place of deep wisdom. A Guru is like a best friend who can see all of your unconscious behavior and point it out to you so you can choose a different option.

Here's an example: A Guru could see you obsessing over a lover who went away. Your mind could be running the same scene over again and again, telling you that if you could have been better in some way, your lover would not have left you. In this scenario, you would likely be suffering greatly, believing that you are bad and do not deserve love. How painful! Gurus can press the pause button on that whole scene. They can say to you, "Hey, your ego is running the show. Why don't you take a moment and see if those thoughts in your head are doing you any good. Maybe you don't need to believe them."

And in that moment of pause, you remember who you are. You gain a new perspective. You get some distance and, as a result, more mastery over your ego's endless strategies to keep you suffering. You can recognize mistakes you made and find forgiveness to move forward. The more you keep coming back to that pause, the stronger your spirit becomes—and the ego curls up in the corner like a puppy dog. God comes rushing into each moment of your life. My only suggestion to you would be to keep your windows open so that the light of the Guru can enter your life.

This chapter will expose the norms our culture tends to believe about Gurus that prevent seekers from discovering the benefits of a Guru. I will offer my perspective on each norm, so you can have both sides of the story. Then you can contemplate the subject of Gurus in your own way—and reach your own conclusions.

A GURU IS DIFFERENT FROM A TEACHER

What's interesting is that there are no synonyms for Guru. You should not confuse a Guru with a teacher, spiritual writer, life coach, or motivational speaker. While there may be innumerable teachers and coaches, Gurus are quite rare.

The title *Guru* is so abused and misused that sometimes the authentic Gurus avoid the title. Anyone can proclaim himself a "Guru." Some wannabe Gurus are simply power-hungry. They will do whatever they can to look like Gurus so they can win influence, make money, or be seen as leaders. But a true Guru has no interest in the pursuits of the ego. A true Guru is interested only in bringing healing and freedom to whoever wants it. Working with a true Guru can transform your life by shining a light on your spiritual path. Progress that could take years—or life-times—to accomplish happens in a miraculously short amount of time.

In a world overloaded with motivational speakers, life coaches, thera-pists, yoga teachers, and self-proclaimed enlightened masters, it has become more important than ever before to understand the true mean-ing of Guru.

NORM 9
I DON'T NEED A GURU

Jack was one of my first contacts when I reached New York. Anyone who spends fifteen minutes with him is impressed by his sparkling personality. He would always start off with his background in drugs and rock-'n'-roll. He would explain how he gained "immense knowl-edge" to cross over and become a sober, successful man. He said he used to be an extremely angry and violent person. "But it's all behind me!" he would say.

But after the first fifteen minutes were over, anyone could see that Jack was a troubled soul.

Although Jack would often mention publicly how he was guided by God and Gurus, he proudly claimed without fail, "Only I am respon-sible for my success! I like to interact with these Gurus because they are nice people. But I don't need one because I have all the power."

He often claimed to control other people's moods and "vibrations," just by the power of his Third Eye. If anyone challenged him, he would get very defensive and point to his fancy cars and house. If anyone did manage to show off more wealth than he had, Jack would reject their success, saying that it will all go away one day because they don't have the same "power" as he does.

Jack never accepted that he needed spiritual guidance. He privately fed money to multiple psychics and clairvoyants to try to control out-comes. But his ego always told him that it's money that gets everything done—not God. Jack loved showing off his spiritual side because it gave him the image of being a nice person. He was quite confident that he was managing the universe. His family and friends would often laugh at his hysterical ideas, but he laughed at them saying that they were not enlightened yet.

The bubble burst one day when legal authorities came after Jack for fraudulent activities in his business, resulting in huge financial losses. He had to sell his car and house, and remain on the go traveling everywhere to find work. Since he had made fun of so many people during his peak, they didn't have much sympathy for him.

Jack is an extreme example of what can happen when someone believes that they do not need a Guru. He was consumed by anger, desire, and jealousy. He was so driven to look like a "successful, spiritual man" that he had no clue who he really was inside. He had no one to show him that his ego was raging out of control.

In some way, our egos trap all of us. When we are overcome by ambition and desire, we lose our inner creativity and end up working only for honors and rewards offered by society. This painful relationship brings out the actor in us. We put on social masks and dance to the tunes of others. The real self gets lost in this blind chase for success.

A lucky few of us feel a deep desire to lose the masks and discover our true nature. But that can be a long and frustrating journey without an experienced, benevolent guide. We do our best to see the strategies of our egos, but we do not have a clear view. We are full of blind spots and defenses.

When we refuse to work with true Gurus, we don't have a clean mirror to hold up in front of our eyes. It's like looking in a dirty mirror to see our face. There is no clarity. We think that we see a smear of chocolate somewhere near our mouth, so we wipe in that general area. But we never know if we got the dirty spot. We are puttering around in confusion. In the same way, we can get lost in the endless twists and turns of the ego. Even if we think we see something important, we never really know for sure. We struggle to change destructive thoughts and behaviors, but we never see through to the root of our suffering. Any changes we try to make are superficial. We use one part of the ego to try to destroy another part of the ego. The part that feels shame about a behavior attacks the part that acts out. And we create an endless loop of suffering.

We might even turn to spiritual teachings, thinking that since they are "spiritual," they must be able to help. We can memorize meditation techniques, but those techniques are irrelevant without a Guru because we are simply picking up whatever our minds think is right. No matter how powerful the technique is, it is worthless if it is carried out by an unclear mind and raging ego. The same is true for reading holy texts. We may read them on our own, but the very minds we are trying to fix come in with arguments and quotes to justify one thought or another. We may feel some mental relief, but it does not last. We do not find healing and conclude that spiritual teachings do not work.

BREAKTHROUGH
YOU NEED TO WITNESS YOU — A GURU IS THE MIRROR

Gurus are like freshly polished mirrors that give us an honest look at ourselves. In comparison to the dirty mirror I discussed earlier, a clean mirror will show us if we have food stuck in our teeth or if our hair is out of control. A true Guru will show us our egos' hidden strategies. They point to the masks and dances directly, without skirting around them. When we see our craziness in a magnifying mirror with an ultra-watt light, we can let it go. We can make space for God to come in.

Here is the secret of true Gurus: The light they shine onto our lives is nothing but a reflection of our own light. A true Guru does not claim to own the light that dispels darkness and illuminates our ego. All they do is hold up a mirror so we can see it for ourselves. This mirror shows us our real self. So a Guru is not giving us something we don't have, just pointing to what we don't see.

But Gurus don't stop there. They will give us cleaning supplies perfectly tailored to clean away our suffering. On our own, we may be trying to remove a soaked-in bloodstain with a feather duster. But a Guru gives us technology to dissolve even the most relentless ego illusions that cloud our awareness.

When a Guru prescribes you a meditation technique or a mantra, it is based upon an evaluation of your energy. Among the hundreds of meditation techniques and mantras, you are given the one that's right for you. You cannot be the doctor and the patient at same time. If you have a minor cough or a cold, you can buy some over-the-counter medicine at a local pharmacy, but it doesn't work if you want to fully heal. You need a specialized doctor to get the problem cured from its roots.

You may have spent thirty years following a path that your parents laid out for you. One day you wake up and desire to follow your own authentic path. But even though you've taken workshops on finding your purpose and met with a coach to set goals, you still don't know where to go. Gurus don't tell you where to go. They can come in and show you your blind spots and give you tools to dissolve them. Then you can see your true path for yourself.

THE PERILS OF GURU DEPENDENCY

I want to address the belief that some seekers develop: believing they always need to have a Guru. This is as damaging as saying, "I don't need a Guru." Imbalanced dependence arises when you end up in the hands of a nutcase "Guru" who makes you feel that you will end up in hell the moment you walk out of their zone. In many cases, they convince you of this so smoothly that you don't realize until the damage has been done. You are made to believe that you need a Guru or else you will be miserable. Some of these so-called Gurus also throw spiritual threats in there, saying that you will be un-blessed and unhappy if you stop seeing them. In any relationship, dependence kills the honor and respect. It squeezes the positive energy out of you. So if a Guru tells you that you will fall apart without him—run!

EXERCISE **ILLUMINATE YOUR BELIEFS ABOUT GURUS**

Working with a Guru has been the most effective, life-altering experience I have ever had. If you want true and lasting transformation, I recommend looking at any beliefs you have that say you don't need a Guru. This exercise will help you to do just that. It encourages you to question your doubts and beliefs about Gurus. There is no right way to answer these prompts. I want you to get a glimpse into your mind.

Write down five reasons why you feel you need a Guru.

Write down five reasons why you feel you don't need a Guru.

Now, have a friend or fellow seeker do the same exercise. Share your responses. Sharing will help you to understand wide views on Gurus and eventually polish your own.

NORM **10**

A GURU IS A MIRACLE

Who doesn't love magic? Objects vanishing and reappearing out of nowhere, tricks that seem impossible —how amusing! Magic shows are great when they are done solely for entertainment. But magic takes a dark turn when it's portrayed as coming from spiritual bliss.

A self-proclaimed Guru can memorize mantras and learn yoga asana just like everyone else, but they may still feel that they are more important than and different from the rest of the teachers out there. Some Gurus try to glorify their title by showing some sort of paranormal power. With emerging technology and education, some old-fashioned tricks are out of business, but there is still so much done to glorify "Guru-ness" by many of the wannabes.

I recently came across a man in a costume (a "Guru") on YouTube who had promised many people that he could awaken Kundalini. I ignored it, thinking it was a joke, but I started seeing other people on my Facebook newsfeed talking about this same thing. These men in costumes get away with selling their magical tricks because there are buyers for them.

During my school years, I watched a documentary featuring a popular Indian Guru. The documentary was focused on the magical stuff that he was most known for. Tricks like producing holy ash from his hands, and many such acts, were common in this Guru's discourses. The documentary became huge news and various publications in India began writing stories claiming that he had sexually harassed some of his devotees.

I never had the chance to meet this Guru when he was alive, but I know many people who don't leave their house without bowing down to his picture. The documentary and the news stories did hurt his popularity, but he is still worshipped globally by countless disciples. I am not one to judge his miracles. I can't perform those tricks. I also haven't done as much charitable work as he has. My only concern is that such a portrayal of miracles tends to distract people from the main goal of the spiritual path, which is self-realization. Showing a trick like producing something from thin air makes a spiritual Guru look like a magician. I don't deny that some rituals may be mystic, but presenting even the simplest thing as mystical takes one away from the authentic truth.

We are too conditioned by the idea that enlightenment cannot happen easily. We think we have to move to the Himalayas or find a Guru who can levitate. Reading your mind is not a sign of enlightenment. Levitation is not a sign of enlightenment. These are simply phases that one can master. But if they tempt you, bliss will be a far-off dream. I want to warn seekers to not be amused by any of these tricks. Your Guru will not appear like Superman. Just like Hollywood fairy tales ruin our romantic ideology, a Guru's real persona is ruined by these stereotypical tales.

When the soul is in misery, it takes solace in whoever promises a solution. If a miracle man offers a solution, then so be it. A huge problem is our impatient nature when it comes to spirituality. Seeking out shortcuts and miracles won't solve anything. We have to realize our laziness to come out of our misery. We have to understand that problems have happened and that we must do deep spiritual work to heal our wounding. Now is the time to resolve. Now is the time to heal.

BREAKTHROUGH
EVERYTHING IS
A MIRACLE

Back in 2004, I had applied to Baruch College in New York City, but I wasn't getting any response to my application. I checked every morning, but there was never a change in status. When I called, they told me to call back after three weeks. Two days after that, I was having breakfast with my dad and he asked me to check on the status. I explained to him what the college officials had told me.

"You are accepted. Call them!" he said, while sipping his favorite Indian masala chai.

I decided to call them right in front of him, just to prove to him that I wasn't accepted yet. I called and the automated message said, "You have been accepted."

I labeled it a miracle.

Just this week, a woman visited our center in New York complaining of headaches, anxiety, and panic attacks. I asked her a few questions and put her into meditation for a half hour. Afterward, I gave her healing and she calmed down right away. Her husband, who had witnessed it all, called it a miracle.

People ask me a lot of questions at my public talks. Some questions are general, but others are very specific. To give them an answer, I sometimes ask them follow-up questions such as, "Do you see a lot of animals in your dreams?" "Did you see the color blue in your meditation?" or "You used to meditate upon Buddha but stopped completely in the last few months. Why?" When I ask such questions, and I'm telling my attendees something only they would know, they are utterly surprised. They call it a miracle.

My *naani* (grandma) never went to school. She doesn't know how to write or read her own name. I showed her how the touch of my thumb can unlock my iPhone. She called it a miracle.

All of these real-life situations make me wonder, what really is a miracle? When something happens that is beyond our understanding, we often call it either bullshit or a miracle, depending on whether we liked it or not. What doctors do is a miracle to me because I am not a person of science. What I do may look like a miracle or complete bullshit to many doctors, depending upon their interest in spirituality. Before airplanes were invented, the idea of traveling via air must have been thought of as either bullshit or a miracle. The person who first drank milk must have been considered a creepy guy who was harassing cows! There is no end to the number of situations that may seem like nonsense until we understand what they really mean.

MIRACLES ARE NORMAL

Making a handkerchief appear out of thin air (and other such acts) is nonsense, and any authentic Guru will completely avoid claiming to perform these tricks. What we need to understand in this norm is that a miracle is nothing more than a concept that we haven't understood yet. When we understand it, it becomes normal. Miracles are normal.

I keep a beautiful example of miracles printed out in my meditation room. It's a story about a Guru who was traveling on an airplane with other passengers. The plane flew into bad weather and hit turbulence. The pilot told the passengers to fasten their seat belts. A few moments later, the plane started to tilt up and down. Panic set in. Some people started praying and promising to donate money if God would save them. Others started screaming their last prayers. The flight attendants were equally panicked.

Now, the Guru who was on this flight is very popular and known to create miracles. People started asking him to create a miracle and save them, but he just sat there silently. The plane became shakier and everyone thought it would crash. People kept repeating prayers and begging the Guru to make a miracle. But the Guru was as silent as their God was. Fortunately, fifteen minutes later, the plane stabilized and landed safely at its destination. The passengers cheered. The pilot walked out happy. However, the Guru didn't get off the plane. He sat in his seat and began his prayers. This went on for a few minutes.

A passenger asked him, "Why the hell are you praying now?! We asked you over and over again to pray, but you didn't even respond! And now you won't even leave the flight without praying? You're crazy!"

The Guru smiled. "Don't you see the problem?" he said. "You were all screaming God's name when you wanted a quick miracle. You only remember God in moments of stress. Otherwise, God is just a happy idea that you borrow from your holy books. The real prayer is a prayer of gratitude. I create miracles because I spend all of my time exchanging unconditional love with the divine. The time to meditate is in joy. This is a special moment."

The secret to recognizing the miracles in our lives involves paying more attention. When we focus on the multiple ways we are blessed, we will tune in to the miracle channel. Suddenly, we will see miracles everywhere. When we understand that what we call miracles in spirituality are not mystic moments, but just results of a certain process, then the magic of life becomes normal. The possibility of a so-called "miracle" begins to seem more probable.

When we understand this norm, we stop becoming impressed by all of the magic acts performed by self-proclaimed Gurus. Those acts distract us from the real deal. People are so impressed with Jesus walking on water, but they ignore the rest of his other stories about healing and forgiveness. Indians talk about Krishna's involvement with mystical powers instead of trying to follow his acts of love and kindness. We should look at either everything or nothing as a miracle. Then we can take ourselves away from the magical temptations and bring ourselves to the real work—self-realization.

EXERCISE ILLUMINATE YOUR BELIEFS ABOUT MIRACLES

Write down things that you've always considered to be miracles.

If you already have a teacher or a Guru, ask yourself if they perform any of these miracles.

If yes, revisit those miracles and write down how you feel about each of them.

NOᴙM 11

ALL GURUS ARE FRAUDS

I heard about a famous therapist in Los Angeles who sent his son abroad to study. The son graduated with honors. Upon his return home as a qualified therapist, he gifted his parents with a month-long trip to Europe. "Dad, you have been working too hard," he said. "Now your relaxation time starts! I will take care of the psychology clinic while you are away."

Any father would be proud of this. Right?

The proud parents went to Europe and returned home hale and hearty. The father's first question for his son upon returning was about how the clinic work had gone.

"Dad, you will be so happy to hear about the progress I made while you were away," the son said. "Remember that young lady from Beverly Hills who had been coming to you for the past few years? She's better now and off of her medication. And that guy from Wall Street who travels to L.A. just to see you? He is off his medication, too, and just needs to follow up in a few months. Oh, and Lisa, who's been in therapy on and off: I asked her to start meditating. She already feels better! And listen to this. . . ."

"Wait!" His father interrupted angrily. "Did you not think that I could fix their problems? Did you think I was dumb to have them in therapy for this long? My son, the lady from Beverly Hills paid for your tuition. The Wall Street client paid off your car. And Lisa's years of therapy got you through the five-star hostel stay. I could have fixed them in a few days, too. But the first rule of our job is to not fix the root. Instead, just keep treating the symptoms. Damn, you need more training!"

We hear a story like this about people who are supposed to help us be happy and extend that to think this about Gurus as well. We tell ourselves, "All Gurus are frauds!"

While psychologists are known to be professionals who are making a living off helping people, the role of Guru is often associated with controversy and scandal. Look up any popular Guru in history, and you will likely find a controversy attached to that person. A major reason for this trouble is that, unlike other professions, like doctors and lawyers, there is no way to certify a Guru. When a Guru rises in authority, they almost always become too power hungry. Sooner or later, the Guru becomes a cult who attracts nothing but fanatics. When a human gets too much power and adoration, almost like a God, ego is impossible to manage. The blind faith of seekers, which makes an authentic Guru humble, makes others pompous.

BREAKTHROUGH
WE ARE RESPONSIBLE FOR FRAUDULENT GURUS

If we have been hurt, abused, or betrayed by our spouses, it doesn't mean that we will never love anyone else. Love is food for our soul. If we build up walls in an attempt to block love, life will cease to exist. Similarly, if we have followed some-one who put on a costume and pretended to be a Guru, that doesn't mean we should stop seeking guidance.

A life without a genuine Guru's grace is like sitting on top of a hidden treasure and never realizing it. Every situation has a positive and negative side. Don't let the negative side bog you down and stop you from reaping the benefits of the positive. When it comes to spiritual guidance, there is too much at stake. Our painful journey can take a U-turn if we start living the life of awareness that a Guru can lead us into.

GIVE UP THE SHORTCUTS

We tend to fall because we want a shortcut. An authentic Guru will make us *work*. They won't feed our ego. Hence, we may not like it at first. Our minds will likely tell us to go elsewhere, where someone else is promising us a miracle. I am not against miracles and faith healing. But I am certainly against spiritual shortcuts.

The temptation to take shortcuts will make it easier for a fraudulent person to exploit us. Spiritual healing doesn't follow shortcuts. In fact, nothing in Mother Nature does. Look at the trees, the mountains, and the seasons. They all take time to evolve. They are not in a hurry. We are.

A Guru will make you uncomfortable, puncture your bloated ego, and make you see yourself without censorship. If you want to manifest to your fullest potential, be ready to give up shortcuts and do the work involved. Spiritual healing comes with no guarantees and no shortcuts.

HOW TO FIND A TRUE GURU

What do you do when you have to buy a new car or a new home? I assume you do research, ask your friends for their opinions, and use your own knowledge to make the right purchase. Even when you buy a new phone or tablet, the decision is based on what you like, what's available, and what suits your style, right? You select your life partner carefully, too. Would you marry a person you didn't like from day one? I hope not.

So, since you have been choosing the most important things in your life based upon research and comfort, you will choose the Guru using the same model, right? You will pick the Guru that you like. You will find solace in the Guru who makes you comfortable. You will seek out the Guru who matches your lifestyle.

Not so fast.

Finding a Guru bears no resemblance to shopping for one. A Guru is not meant to make us feel more comfortable. They arrive in our lives to push our buttons and ignite transformation. So we can't go from place to place, looking for the "right fit." When we decide that we are ready for a Guru, the best thing we can do is begin to work on our egos.

The biggest roadblock to meeting a true Guru is the ego. Remember, you can think of *ego* as standing for "edging Guru out." Take the Guru out, and the ego will walk in. Allow the ego in, and the Guru will walk out. The ego stops us from accepting the idea that someone with flesh and bones can teach us life lessons.

The popular phrase "A teacher appears when a student is ready" is absolutely true in this situation. The ultimate truth is this: *You cannot find a Guru. You can only let a Guru discover you. The only thing you can do is prepare yourself for the Guru's discovery.* Try as much as you want. If you go out and search for a Guru, you may land at a place where your ego is fed.

The title of this section is somewhat of a trick for your ego and shopping habits. But I am not trying to deceive you. I just want you to have clarity. You are much too precious to end up in the wrong hands.

HOW TO *RECOGNIZE* A TRUE GURU

Since I can't teach you how to go out and shop for a Guru, I want to talk about how you can recognize a Guru when one appears in your life. Below you will find a list of traits that all true Gurus share. Please note that these signs will be visible to you *only* after you surrender your ego, or at least start to put your ego aside.

A True Guru Offers Solutions That Require You to Grow

A Guru's solutions are not a standard kind of answer to a problem. No Guru will give you an easy solution. There is nothing more crippling for a spiritual seeker than getting a fix without working for it. I was once told that a Guru would never quench your thirst by giving you answers. Instead, they will make you question yourself more, so that you are inspired to find the answers on your own. I agree completely!

I grew up listening to people tell me that I would never have to work hard because my dad and grandpa are such gifted Gurus. They almost had me convinced that I was the next Superman. But the reality soon kicked in after my dad told me that he would never give me a ready-to-go solution. In fact, he made me wait five years to receive my first mantra, just so that I could understand the value of what I was learning. It took a little more than five years to get my first meditation bead, too.

The solutions that come from a Guru are not based upon any preconceived notions. They are created as you evolve. A Guru questions your solutions and helps you create authentic answers to your life problems.

A Guru Helps You Realize Your Responsibility

Since now there are machines replacing humans, we are not held responsible for ourselves as much as before. I don't meet a human when I deposit or withdraw money from the bank, nor is there any human checking me in at airports. I can deposit checks through my phone or ATM and get my boarding pass in my smartphone's app. There are many more such situations where we simply talk to machines and get the job done. This "devil may care" attitude isn't good. When there is no responsibility, there is no accountability. We cannot evolve into a raised consciousness until we take responsibility for our actions. We can blame the president, the government, our parents, society, or religion, but ultimately we must resolve our own issues. Blame doesn't help anything.

A Guru makes you realize your responsibility by letting you steer your own journey. A Guru's job is to make you a tough seeker, able to face any challenge in life. A pampered kid often turns out to be too soft for the world, while a kid who has had it rough has a better chance of being successful because they have been through challenges. Spiritual enlightenment comprises intense experiences. These experiences grow beautifully when a seeker is ready to take the responsibility of a spiritual path. According to a Guru, your responsibility is not just limited to your daily actions. It goes far beyond that. Everything we do in this lifetime—every success and failure—is the outcome of our actions and intentions. Responsibility means the ability to respond to life. It doesn't mean what others expect you to do. That's conditioning, not responsibility. A Guru teaches you to eventually respond with no fears. As a result, you become spontaneous and understand the real melody of life.

A True Guru Must Be Alive

A Guru must be alive. I mean alive enough to hug you and psychologically kick you when you need it. When the Guru is physically absent, others become successors and interpret the Guru's teachings their own way. Today, we don't have Buddha, Mohammed, Krishna, or Jesus, but I can vouch that they did not mean to say some of what is interpreted as their teachings.

When a Guru is alive, there is vibrancy. There is freedom and yet a management of the journey. All of the Guru's books and teachings lose their meaning right after their physical body passes on because a Guru lives in the present. The past and future are irrelevant to a Guru. Their solution to the same problem may change over time because the student's energy, or even the world's energy, may change as time passes, too. A Guru responds to the present moment, not to past information.

I always say that if you find a Guru, never ever leave. While a Guru is alive, they can teach you to discover the God in you. When the Guru is gone, you may start a religion or a nonprofit foundation in the Guru's name, but the opportunity is gone. Later, you will simply live on past memories. Of course, there are many Gurus who keep guiding their seekers even when their physical bodies cease to exist. But my suggestion is to get the work done while your Guru is still alive. Afterlife teaching sessions work only for the seekers who were already working on higher planes when the Guru was physically present.

A True Guru Wants You to Be Independent

When you were a child, your parents held your hands to help you walk. Do they still do that? I assume not. At some point, they had to let you walk on your own. Of course, you probably fell a few times, but you stood back up. They made sure you weren't hurt but also made sure you were not too dependent on them. Parents who make their children over-dependent cripple them, physically or mentally. A Guru who makes you dependent and doesn't let you go spiritually cripples you.

A True Guru Goes Beyond Religion

A Guru's message goes beyond religion and all other popular norms. Gurus don't repeat heavy quotes from scriptures; instead, they guide you from experience. A Guru will accept you in your religion. There won't be a need to convert into anything. In the 1960s in Northern India, my grandfather always had students from all religions and faiths. My father's students and clients vary and are from different cultures. He suggests prayers from their own faiths. I learned the same openness from him. A large majority of my students are non-Hindus. There has never been a discussion on religion or conversion. In my experience with many other Gurus, their openness toward religion has always been very positive. Someone who has truly understood the meaning of divine love wouldn't waste time on the differences among religions.

If you come across someone who promises you some heaven of happiness by converting to a different faith, be careful. Conversion of religion doesn't do anything. Transformation of being does everything. This transformation doesn't need to beg any religion. It can happen with or without religion if a seeker is ready to surrender onto a Guru's path.

A True Guru Will Dismantle Your Ego

A Guru will attack your ego from many angles. You can either take these attacks as insults or learn to understand the hidden lessons in them. The problem is that we're programmed in such a way that any simple method to cure the ego doesn't work. Society, schools, and parents feed our ego. One person, a Guru, wants to detoxify you from all of the ego clutter. It is a lot of work, but it can be done if you apply yourself.

•

As you can see, I think working with a true Guru is one of the most beneficial things a seeker can do. A Guru can see your blind spots, push your buttons, and break through your ego. A Guru is the most direct path to God in this lifetime. If you are curious about the Guru relationship, simply hold the intention to gain greater clarity. If you feel a strong desire to meet a Guru, you can follow the exercise below. I cannot guarantee that a Guru will discover you, but I can certainly help you prepare yourself for that most auspicious meeting. The points I made in this chapter will help you to discern the true Gurus from the fakes.

EXERCISE **MAKE YOURSELF READY FOR A GURU**

This exercise is an invitation to be an observer of yourself. When you contemplate your actions and decisions, do you think they are under the influence of ego or love?

In your journal, answer the following questions:
- What offends you? How quickly do you get offended?
- Do you judge others easily?
- Do you take time to reflect upon the choices you make every day?

Before you start your meditation, add this intention: "My intention is to make myself ready for the Guru who will accept me as a seeker. The universe and God are making me ready for my Guru every day in every way."

Now begin your meditation practice.

Continue to focus on your own ego, and send this intention out to the universe. The Guru will appear when you are ready.

RISING IN LOVE

Years back, I met a friend who was in his late thirties. After we talked about weather, politics, and movies, the discussion turned to love and relationships.

"So, when are you getting married?" I asked him.

"Not yet," he answered. "I'm looking for the perfect one. You know, Miss Right!"

I asked nothing more and we headed out for dinner. Several years later, I ran into him randomly at a family function. I had to ask if he ever met "Miss Right."

"I did!" he exclaimed. "She was all that I imagined her to be: gorgeous, flawless, and it just felt so right."

"Where is she?" I asked. I looked around curiously to see if I could recognize her in the crowd. "When are you getting married? Or are you already married?"

"We're not married," he answered. "She said no. She was looking for Mr. Right and he wasn't me."

This story illustrates the norms we have been taught around love. We believe that love comes in a particular form, in a particular way. While we are all busy chasing this Mr. or Miss Right, the result is that we keep the love we seek away. We never realize the pure love we all crave.

On our walks through life, we crave many things. The desire for love is the strongest craving of all. Everyone has an intense need for love: a newborn baby, an eighty-year-old grandpa, or even a prisoner who has committed a heinous crime. Just as your physical body needs food to survive, the soul needs a healthy dose of love to live.

But the problem is that we have collectively put love in a box. We live our lives on the principles taught to us by society, religion, government, teachers, and parents. Love is the most misunderstood among them all. The damage that has been done in the name of love is irrecoverable. The phrase *I love you* has become a mantra that has the ability to penetrate and exploit a person's heart. Once meaningful, it is now often reduced to an empty statement.

FALLING IN LOVE

There is a simple reason why we fall in love so easily: falling is always easy. Whether you jump from a five-foot platform or a fifty-foot building, it will take only a few seconds for you to reach the ground. And while the fall into love isn't equal to falling from a building, it's a fall that has tempted many souls throughout history. Love looks inviting and amazing on the other side of the fall, and we forget everything so we can leap.

If you jump from a skyscraper, you'll feel nothing but air until you hit the ground. The problem starts when the falling stops. The moment you hit the ground, it hurts, and the fall is likely bad enough to put an end to your life. I apologize for giving you such a gruesome image of falling in love, but it's time we all face the real problem.

Fairy tales have made falling in love sound fancy, but in real life, the problems are real. Many of us hold a fantasy about what romantic love will look and feel like. You may think your "soul mate" will have a perfect body, be smart and successful, with the potential to earn a substantial income. You may expect this person to understand you completely, to accept your faults, delight you in the bedroom, and meet all of your emotional needs. And, of course, this person will want to marry you!

But what often happens is that people project this fantasy of perfection onto whoever they may be dating. The fantasy mixes with endorphins and the desperate desire to be loved. These ingredients form a powerful elixir that intoxicates. Falling, even jumping into love seems like a divine thrill. But then we wake up and see that our ideas about what love "should" look like are not what we fell into.

At this point, we may feel anger, resentment, doubt, and even despair. We think, "How can my beloved be so flawed? Where is my *real* soul mate?"

RISING IN LOVE

Instead of falling in love, we need to rise in love. We need to evolve beyond our limiting beliefs about love's nature. We need to understand that love is much more than our templates of soul mates, marriage, family, and children. These ideas have been corrupted throughout generations by religions, media, families, and all of society.

Here's an example of how ridiculous this corruption can get: In some traditions, you are not allowed to touch a woman before marriage. Yet you are allowed to have brutal sex on your wedding night. That is not marriage. That is rape that goes unnoticed. There are plenty of people out there who believe that such behavior is an acceptable expression of "love."

My point is that anyone can define love in any way, whether or not that definition is true. Love's true nature cannot be defined. That's because love is free. Love is free because love *is* the divine, and the divine is certainly free.

Our longing for love, and our longing for God, are the same. When we love another, we are touching God in that person. Likewise, loving humans is training for loving the divine. Rising in love means bringing our tired, old definitions of love into the light of God. Instead of falling for the illusions, we rise to the occasion of love's true invitation.

We will know we have accepted love's invitation because we will be free from pain. Love has constantly been burdened with accusations that it causes miserable pain. These pains are not of love. These pains are the illusions that we have labeled as love. To fall in love means we identify a person who we think will live up to illusions of a perfect object of our affection. When they can't, we feel pain. That's because we are putting conditions on love. But love is not only free—it is unconditional.

Rising in love means seeing love unconditionally in all of creation. There is no pain in love when we accept each moment unconditionally.

How could there be? Acceptance is the pathway to freedom—and to authentic love. When we accept ourselves and those around us, we connect to divine love.

RISE TO BECOME YOUR TRUE SELF

Rising in love starts with you. It is an invitation to unpack the norms you have absorbed and clarify what love truly means in your own heart. It does no good to read about love and move on to the next part of your day. Each of us must make the inquiry into love's true nature for ourselves.

If you have doubts about love, give them your attention. Doubts are probably in your mind because of your conditioning. Meditate on them and eventually a beautiful clarity will envelop you. This clarity is your true nature, free of doubts. Meditating upon doubts doesn't mean giving them more energy. When we meditate upon something, we witness its true nature. We don't get attached or identified with it. Rather we move beyond its grip on us. I meditate upon my fears and self-doubts. Doing this helps me to understand that my doubts are nothing more than my self-created illusions. They start to vanish when I observe them with mindful energy.

True love is an experience that makes you empty enough that you can fill yourself with the divine. The ego lives in our head. But love dwells in the center of our being, in our heart. The light of love shines from our center into our darkest places, and when it does, those places can't hold us back anymore. In this way, it kills our egos. It makes us surrender our shallow identities so that we can rise to become our true selves. In order to experience this emptiness, I suggest you be more mindful of your emotions. The ego tells us not to be vulnerable. Yet we find ourselves in moments when we can't resist crying, laughing, and feeling the lovely love. One way to really see this happening in you is to acknowledge your heart center in meditation. Meditating upon the heart will help to release fears and repressed emotions. The key is to not judge any emotions. Simply let them flow.

When the ego gets out of the way, we know that love is not what we say or do. Love is who we are.

If you are not expressing love, you are not being yourself. You will find that your true self is made of nothing but love. This is the true meaning of "self-love." When you witness your flaws and your demons without judging them, you realize immense compassion at the core of your being. The energy of this self-compassion is your true nature. It comes from within to feed your soul first, and then it can't help but overflow.

Just like our body needs food to survive and stay healthy, our soul needs self-love to stay healthy. Not being able to love ourselves has damaging consequences. One can feel lonely, depressed, and unworthy of happiness. Individuals lacking in self-love often struggle to form healthy relationships in life. Self-love doesn't have a method or technique. It has to become a quality, a state of our consciousness. Self-love doesn't need validation from others. You will surely face your inner demons as you cultivate the state of self-love, but do not feed them. Do not get identified with your fears and don't defend or run away from them either. Be the observer of this process.

The following three norms are prevalent misconceptions in our culture, which make us doubt that free, unconditional love is our true nature. As you read, give yourself time to contemplate each one for yourself. Otherwise, my words will only add another layer to your conditioning. We each must make the endeavor to discover true love in our own way. I hope the following insights guide you to ask questions about love that are relevant to you. Then you can rise in love.

NORM 12
WE POSSESS THE PEOPLE WE LOVE

When we meet a person who evokes feelings of love and joy in our hearts, it's common to want to hold on to that person. We think, "If that person leaves my life, love will leave my life."

I see plenty of people who are insecure because they fear their potential partner will leave them for something better. They just want to secure their bond. Many people get married just to make sure that they can lock in something good. We are taught to possess everything in order to make it ours. We are made to sign possession papers in order to secure the property we buy. Such rules are only helpful in material things and create havoc in matters of love. Relationships based on possession only end up doing one thing perfectly: possessing each other.

I often wonder at the mindset of the person who invented the idea of marriage. He must have murmured, "I love you. I really do. And I love you so much that I want government, religion, and society to make you mine. Only mine."

But does a legal marriage secure the affections of your beloved? Not necessarily. Even if you have a legal document securing your bond with your spouse, that is certainly no guarantee that your relationship will never end. Love doesn't follow rules we project onto it. We may be so busy making sure that a relationship lasts forever that we lose the present joy it has to offer. And when we try to make someone a slave to our emotions or needs, we will never get what we are after. We will get a pretension, or a love that is not real. The quality of the relationship is corrupted.

We either crave to possess someone or crave to be possessed because we crave security. The possession could mean controlling or demanding that our partners act in a certain way. We may feel a sort of ownership in our relationships. This is damaging, to say the least, to any relationship. This possession, be it in a romantic or non-romantic relationship, gives us an illusion that the other person belongs only to us. But possession can never make us secure. The irony is that when we try to possess love, we keep it away. This possession ruins whatever possibility there was for love. That's because if we don't let go and allow unconditional love, we cannot heal at a deep level.

Only unconditional love makes us truly secure. True love is the most potent healing force there is. It's the medium that breaks through our conditioning so we can know our truth. Sometimes God or meditation gets the credit for healing, but both of those concepts are about accessing pure love.

BREAKTHROUGH

LOVE AND FREEDOM GO HAND IN HAND

Remember earlier in the chapter when I said love is free? Well it's true! You can't predict or control love. When we finally admit that we can't control love by placing demands on our partners, we can realize that love is alive in each moment. This is the pure, unconditional presence that we all really want. It is so much bigger than any concepts we may believe about security or permanence. And when we trust that power, we can give up our attempts at control or possession. We see that love flows effortlessly, without our strategies.

It's such a relief to let love be free! When we admit that love is in charge, we can relax. We can admit that love has more intelligence than we do. And it will hold us even if we mess up—and even if our love objects leave our lives.

I invite you to remove your claws from everyone you love. Those claws may be obvious. Maybe you are always nagging your partner, waiting for them to marry you. Or maybe the claws are subtler. Maybe you feel anxious every time your partner goes out with friends. Any anxiety over what your loved one will or won't do, as well as any attempts to control the outcome of your relationship, is clawing against the flow of life.

Letting go of possession is ultimately about *you* and *your* freedom. When you are preoccupied with whether someone else will be with you for a certain amount of time, you can't see your own purpose. You can't feel the unconditional love that lives in each moment. You are creating your own suffering. So remove your claws, release your strategies. Open to the love that is *here,* regardless of anything—or anyone—else. Then we can all be love worshippers instead of object worshippers.

FREEDOM + UNCONDITIONAL LOVE = GROWTH

Unconditional love is also the secret ingredient to growth. If we try to keep our loved ones under our thumbs, they will feel stunted, unsatisfied, and unexpressed. They won't have the freedom to be who they truly are. They won't have a chance to try things and make mistakes. But when we give up our definitions of how our loved ones "should" be, they can grow into the purpose-driven, passionate, enlivened people they are meant to be. And we can, too.

I am married to a wonderful lady who is my biggest strength in life. In Indian marriage tradition, you walk around the sacred fire in seven rounds promising to live together in love and protect each other. When my wife's and my seven rounds were complete, I looked over at her and asked her to take an eighth round, to promise that we would never let our marriage interfere in our love.

Since then, we have lived each day as it comes to us. I am married, and yet I am not living within the defined laws of it. For me, the most important part of our bond is our freedom and allowing each other to find the meaning of that freedom. It has worked out very well for us so far. There may be a day when it will stop working out, but who knows? We have promised each other not to project love or any fancy story, and we have merged our colors with each other, all without losing our original colors.

EXTRAMARITAL AFFAIRS? ENGAGE THE URGE

In Indian culture, it is a sin and taboo to get divorced or denounce a marriage. This taboo has resulted in countless suppressed relationships and an endless stream of extramarital affairs.

Just know that whatever you suppress will bounce back. It is perfectly fine to be attracted to someone else while you are married. There is no denying it. You come across someone who has a charming personality and you admire them. This admiration may result in a deep liking for the person. People who claim that they are never attracted to anyone else while they are in a relationship are fooling themselves. It is natural to admire beauty. If you deny it or run away from it, someone else will come along sooner or later and the same thing will happen.

You may even fall for a person and have what we call an extramarital affair. These affairs happen because you are trying to chase something. Sex doesn't need love to make it happen. You have a thirst that has yet to be quenched. It could be simply a hunger for sex or for a fresh energy. My suggestion is to explore it further. Don't be scared of it. Don't stop it. Whatever action you choose, be very aware of what you are doing. Ask yourself deeper questions and answer them with utmost honesty. Is it time to leave your marriage? Is this extramarital affair just a break from your monotonous life? Or does this feel like another long journey of love? I am not one to judge you. But I want you to ask yourself those questions while you are on this "break" from your marriage.

If you decide to go this way, make your intentions clear to your partner. Any relationship with lies and dishonesty will head to ruin. But a harsh truth sometimes clears up many misunderstandings. I am not suggesting that you dive into "open relationships" necessarily, where you constantly move from partner to partner. My intention is to make you and your partner aware of any issues. The desire for an affair could come from a lack of a friendship between you and your partner. Whatever the issue, it must be talked about fearlessly. Yes, your partner may not take your honesty positively and the relationship may end. But it isn't having its best ride anyway if you can't talk about such an important issue.

Many temptations to stray are often disengaged during meditations. When we engage them and mindfully handle our emotions, we may realize we do not really want to act them out. A spiritual mentor or even a good friend's support in such situations can help you to sail through the situation well. Remember, love doesn't need sex for its survival. Make your moves wisely.

EXERCISE **ACCEPT YOUR PARTNER UNCONDITIONALLY**

This exercise is suggested for couples, right before you go to sleep at night.

Clean your bedroom. Put fresh sheets on the bed and light an aromatic candle.

Sit across from each other. Take a few deep breaths.

Gaze into each other's eyes. Touch each other's fingertips. Continue to touch fingertips and breathe together.

Open yourself to love and healing for one another.

Visualize yourself as a reservoir of love and pour love into each other.

Continue for ten minutes.

NORM 13
ANOTHER PERSON
CAN MAKE US WHOLE

"You complete me."

"I feel one with you."

"We are complete now that we are married."

The widespread and unconscious use of such romantic lines is seriously damaging our heart chakras, friends. I am not kidding. The whole idea of relationships in these statements is built upon dependence on a second party. We are taught to believe that if only we could find our "soul mates," life would fall into place and we would finally be happy. This idea is so strongly engrained in us that we constantly feel left out, or like something is missing in our lives, until we are in relationships.

The problem with this collective illusion is that it makes it normal to avoid taking responsibility for ourselves. No one wants to clean their inner self, but everyone wants the perfect person to swoop in and fill their voids. Lots of singles look to heal themselves from a childhood pain or recover from a past abusive relationship through whomever they may be dating. Instead of facing our demons and working to heal our wounds, we think, "When I meet my perfect partner, I will not feel my pain anymore."

If we are in a relationship, we may think there is someone better "out there," who will make us happy and complete. Since our current partners are not making us feel whole, they must be the wrong partners.

In my perspective, every relationship is a mirror. Whatever bothers you about your partner is a reflection of a part of yourself that you have not yet learned to love. So if you are leaving your spouse, you may be running away from yourself. It won't solve the problem. There was a reason you got together. If you have been able to figure out why the relationship isn't working, then you can move on. But if you are just calling it quits because things have gotten ugly, then it's the ugliness in *you* that really needs the cleansing.

When we believe someone "out there" will complete us, we overlook what is *right here*. We miss the authentic love that is present in every moment. Without knowing the unconditional love that lives within our own hearts, regardless of objects or circumstances, we keep believing that we need a perfect partner to make us whole. It's the external searching itself that distracts us and keeps us from finding the authentic love we truly seek—the love that is already *here*.

BЯEAKTHЯOUGH
YOU AND ONLY YOU CAN MAKE YOURSELF WHOLE

I was walking down Hollywood Boulevard the other day. I live just a few blocks away, and sometimes I purposely take this crowded route so I can watch the tourists yearning for Hollywood glamour—and also the vendors cashing in on their yearning. It is quite an interesting sight.

What makes it even more interesting is the sight of the homeless people who set up shop on various corners. They scream, hold up funny signs, and do all kinds of things to gain attention for money and food. On my walk this particular day, I saw two homeless people sitting next to each other displaying their fancy signs to tourists. Whenever each would receive something, they would immediately put it in their personal bag. They could only hope to get food and money from people walking by them—not from each other. Why? Because obviously they were both homeless and had very little so they could only give each other what they already had. Right?

If you think the answer to the question I just asked is very obvious, then you have figured out the formula of a relationship: *You can only give something to your significant other if you already have it.*

Do you seek love from your partner because you don't have it? What if it turns out that your better half is also seeking the same love from you? It is just like two homeless people seeking *home* from each other. They will both never have it unless one builds it and then helps the other one build it, too.

You cannot become whole by adding someone else to your life. No one can come from the outside and make you feel fulfilled on the inside. Only you can make yourself whole. When we are whole in ourselves, we are complete. That means we can live our full potential as human beings. Instead of holding back, we can express our love and our pain fully, without shame. We can be completely happy and truly free.

Living wholly is related to living holy. Holiness means being the complete spectrum of who you are. That means you feel free to be angry or sad, and also full of love and joy—even if you are afraid. It has nothing to do with temples or churches.

You don't have to take my word for it, but ask yourself how many people you have chased to make yourself feel complete up until now. And let me ask you: How many times have you been successful at it? You will do yourself a great favor by working on making yourself a complete being first. Only then will you attract a person who's as complete as you are. Until then, this cycle will never end.

DISCOVERING YOUR WHOLENESS

People who have not lived completely surround us each day. Many people in our lives—our teachers, parents, and community—have transferred what they know onto us. So we don't know what really living looks like. It is unknown and scary.

That's where meditation comes in. Daily meditation is the number one way to realize wholeness in yourself. That's because our practice breaks through our fears of being whole. It uncovers the wholeness that is always in our hearts.

The truth is, we are born whole, and nothing could ever diminish that fact of our true nature. What happens is this: We learn lies that our ego tells us that cover our wholeness. We learn shame, fear, and stories of lack. And those lies become the lenses through which we see the world and ourselves.

But when we meditate, we clean house. All the fears and false stories diminish, so the brightness of our perfection can shine through. Instead of looking for love outside, meditation gives us the concrete experience that we are made of love—whole, complete, and without end.

WANTING LOVE IS NOT THE CURE—SHARING LOVE IS

You can demand love from your spouse, family, and friends—you can even try to find it online—but this love from others will not solve anything. I have been working in Hollywood for a while, and I have met many seekers who receive plenty of love and applause from the public. But they are not happy. They have immense wealth, and yet they still feel something is missing.

On the other hand, I come across many celebrities who help people in a big way. They understand that seeking love isn't the solution. The solution is in sharing the love. There have been so many suicides in Hollywood due to depression. Do you think it was because those celebrities didn't have enough people screaming their names out loud? Or because they didn't have enough wealth? Depression took over because they were too late in sharing the love they had in them.

We all have it. You don't have to be a celebrity to share your love. You can do it in any small way you can.

We are conditioned to believe that love is about receiving. But love is about giving. Sharing love means giving mutual respect and allowing others to grow in their way. It means helping each other to find meaning instead of pushing a meaning that contains our egos' hidden ulterior motives, programmed into us by media, society, and the environment.

And here is the irony of giving love: To fully give from a place of unconditional acceptance, we must be an open space. That's because true love is a field of infinite happiness. Sharing love has everything to do with being conscious of this open space, which lives in each moment, in each of us. You could do nothing but sit in silence, and if you are empty—with your attention on openness—you are giving love. Can you see how giving love in this way is free from agenda? Free from any covert strategies of control?

I want you to know that sharing love never looks a certain way. Whatever arises in the space of emptiness and truth is a form of love. That can mean saying, "No." It can also mean letting go of a partner when the relationship has reached its natural conclusion. It is not about heart-shaped valentines and perfect rosebuds. When you have the intention to share love in whatever form it chooses to take, you will have confidence, spontaneity, and creativity in your actions. Plus, you will never run out of love to give and you will never feel depleted.

EXERCISE **RELEASE INSECURITY AND ACCEPT YOURSELF**

Doing this exercise daily for ten minutes will help you release the insecurity and anxiety associated with your self-image. As a result, you will develop a comfortable relationship with your existence and accept yourself wholly.

Find a spot to meditate and sit comfortably. Take few deep breaths.

Bring your awareness to your navel. Your navel is your center; it is your universe. Keeping your awareness on your navel helps you regain power. Pay attention to your navel for a few moments.

Inhale. Hold your breath for few moments. Slowly exhale. Continue for ten minutes.

NORM 14
LOVE IS ABOUT GETTING WHAT WE WANT

"I want you."

"I need you."

"I desire you."

We often confuse love with these statements. A wife often stays happy as long as she gets nice gifts, weekly dates, and all of the other relationship "perks." The moment this stops, she may feel ignored or unloved. The husband often stays happy as long as the wife satisfies his physical and emotional needs without any interruption. This cycle has quite a high success rate because both people in a relationship are happy when they get their wants fulfilled. The problem occurs when one party stops or gets bored with the pattern. The moment this exchange of goods stops, the so-called "love" also stops. Over time, the love between couples is reduced to just the demands and desires they put on each other.

Sure, you can keep satisfying your needs—sex, outings, parties, gifts, emotions—but eventually it will all come to a standstill. How long can you continue to feed yourself on these same monotonous things?

One of my friends is a relationship coach in Los Angeles, and he tells me that in a relationship, most men seek sex and most women seek emotional support. As long as they both keep getting what they need, the relationship has a high chance of survival. My question to him was, among sex and emotional needs, where is the unconditional love?

Believing that love should give us what we want is rooted in the ego. As you will recall from chapter 4, one way *ego* can be defined is "edging God out."

When ego walks in, godliness ceases to exist. Ego tempts the mind and thrives on power trips. It gets its food in terms of promises and commitments that will never happen. We let ourselves stay on this ego ride because we are hearing what we want to hear in the moment. The ego stays in power when we believe that we need our partners to give us what we want.

BREAKTHROUGH
LOVE IS ALL ABOUT GIVING

When you root your awareness in the authentic love that lives in you, as you, everything changes. Instead of searching for someone to give you what you don't have, complete you, and make you happy, you realize that you don't need anything to change in order to feel love. I'm not saying that all pain instantly disappears. You may still notice the pull of your ego's illusions, but you won't get caught in the lies. The reaching and grasping slows down, and you find that true love is overflowing in each moment. In fact, there is more love available than you could ever need. You feel such fullness, that instead of trying to get more love, the natural result is to *give* the love.

I'm also not saying that love means having to sacrifice yourself. I am not here to make you feel like a martyr in love—that will only add another feather to the ego crown you are wearing. What I mean is that love means surrendering your ego and giving in to love without making any fuss about it.

The giving should not be an effort, but rather a way of life for you. Try giving your love to someone, and you will be amazed with its power. If giving love feels draining, it is probably not love that you are giving. If you check, you will likely see that your ego was still controlling the show at a subtle level. You may have been giving some imitation of love, while still subtly trying to get something for yourself.

Only true love knows how to give. It doesn't know how to take. The most visible form of this type of love is seen between a child and a mother. No matter how many mistakes children make, mothers will always forgive. They can't stay angry for too long. If you want to learn unconditional love, learn it from a mother and a child.

My *naani* (grandma) taught me the selfless nature of true love. When I was in India, in the eleventh grade, my sleeping schedule was quite irregular. I would stay awake all night and sleep in late. Sometimes I would fall asleep around 7 p.m. and wake up at 3 a.m. to study. My naani asked me what I would have when I was hungry at night. I told her that I would just warm up whatever was cooked for dinner.

"No way," she said painfully. "Why would you eat food that's not fresh? Especially when you are studying so hard!"

I told her that the food was still fresh and it really wasn't that old, but she disagreed. She decided to sleep in the room across from mine. When I turned my light on around 2 a.m., she would get up and make my favorite dish for me. It wasn't just for a night or two—this went on for *two years*. If you asked her, she probably wouldn't even remember. It was not an effort for her. She did it out of unconditional love. My naani's only wish has been to see me happy. My happiness makes her happy. I have learned the meaning of love from her.

Even while writing this memory about her, I am teary-eyed thinking of her grace. It's the power of her love that brings a tear to my eyes sitting seven seas away. In addition, my parents and my better half have given the epitome of love to me. It really rewires your consciousness if your family and loved ones offer you unconditional love. It secures you in a way. It gives you enough strength to take on any challenge.

BE THE LOVE

If you feel that you don't have anyone in your life giving you unconditional love, then be the one who gives unconditional love to others. Love attracts more love, and giving attracts generosity. So focus on how you can give, share, and multiply the love that lives in each moment.

Always remember to check and make sure that your giving is coming from the place of abundant emptiness inside yourself. If there is any guilt, shame, fear, or obligation, your action is probably not really coming from love. And those actions will likely produce suffering down the road. But when your actions spring from deep within the ocean of your heart, you will never have to clean up the mess you made in your attempts to be a martyr. You will find the appropriate form of love to give in each moment.

You see, being love is as simple as being yourself.

EXERCISE **UNCOVER EGO'S HIDDEN AGENDAS IN YOUR RELATIONSHIP**

This exercise is designed for you to travel to the dark lanes of your love life. Don't attempt to do this until you feel comfortable and brutally honest with yourself. Because we keep our pains hidden, talking about them or even writing about them reveals some deep truths. Do this when your mind is fresh. Avoid doing it when you are in stress, anger, or excited about something in relation to your love matters. Give your mindful attention to it.

Write down a list of things you get from your spouse or partner that you wish to get.

Look carefully through the list and see why you need each of the things you mentioned.

In an honest moment with yourself, eliminate each of these things from the list.

Now, picture yourself with your loved one without any of the things that you had desired to get from them. Do you still feel the same love for your spouse? The answer is a revelation for you so you can better understand your love.

FROM KAMA SUTRA
TO CALM SUTRA

There once was a man who was confused about sex. He grew up in a small town in India, where the only college in the city prohibited girl-boy conversations, punishing it by a fine of a hundred rupees. The town also had a narrow view on dating. There were hardly any public displays of affection. The people in the town weren't uneducated or cruel in any way. In fact, it was one of the more developing towns in the area. It had simply adopted this lifestyle from a conservative attitude of suppression.

The young man could have easily adopted this lifestyle, too, but he had a habit of reading to acquaint himself with the rest of the world. He also loved Bollywood (Indian cinema) and Hollywood cinema. Books and media from outside his town portrayed sex in its glorified form. He saw images of men and women achieving transcendent ecstasy and perfect union through sex. The man got more and more confused until it was time for him to move to New York to get a higher education. Once there, he realized that while his small town was too conservative, New York was probably too casual about sex. If he saw many restrictions on public displays of affection or even open dating in his small town, New York displayed the opposite. There, the city dwellers joyfully expressed affection in public and frequented websites to make dating happen. While his town in India considered marriage to be the final destination of romance, New York didn't seem too fond of it. New York was okay about rotating non-committal relationships, with sex as the main goal. It was quite a culture shock. Stuck in two worlds, he found solace in Tantra.

The man spent hours, days, and months understanding Tantra and its life-altering view on sex. Soon, the young man found himself in a much more comfortable space. He not only helped others to understand sex better, but also began to understand sex as a form of higher energy.

That young man has now penned a full chapter on sex in his book. If you haven't guessed already, I am the man I've been writing about. My process of understanding sex wasn't an overnight enlightenment. During my teenage years, a perverted view of sex had certainly caught me when every friend of mine had fascinations with porn. Not that I hated to watch it, but I knew it was not the right way to satisfy the sexual urge.

The practical meditations and a daily evolution of consciousness helped me so much in my own life. This understanding of sex also paved the way for me to help clients who struggle with deep relationship issues with roots in how they deal with sex.

Sex is an essential part of all of us. We were born from sex. Sex keeps the human race on the planet. But our understanding of sexuality is often clouded and distorted. Not many of us experience the true bliss of sex. That's because sex is taboo in our culture. We are simply not taught how to engage with our sexual urges in a conscious way. Many of us are even raised to believe that sex is sinful or shameful. I was educated by Catholic nuns, so believe me, I get the pain of that view.

We have seven centers of energy in our bodies, called chakras, which correspond to different aspects of life. Our sexual energy is contained in the lowest chakra of the body, the *muladhara* chakra, which is located in the pelvis. When this lowest chakra is open and clear, we experience creativity, flow, connection, pleasure, and relaxation. However, when that energy gets stuck in the pelvis, it can create difficulties.

Energy gets stuck in the muladhara chakra because our culture sends confusing messages about sex. At some level, I believe that most people try to repress or mishandle their sexual energy because they don't know what else to do. In the absence of quality guidance, ignoring or hiding from the potency of sexual desire seems like the easiest way to handle it.

From the day we are born, we cannot resist the attraction we have toward sex. The more we try to ignore it or repress it, the harder it persists. We are widely taught to resist the expressions of many emotions, be it crying, laughing, or even loving. So we tend to live them on a partial basis. We never truly step into the full experience of them, or let them affect us. The same is true for sexuality.

Repression causes us to press the desire. It means not looking at sexual energy with compassion, but hiding it under the carpet. Repression is running away from the problem. On the spiritual journey, if we hold any resistance toward sexual energy, it will become trapped and stagnant in the pelvis, which blocks our energy from reaching the upper chakras and, therefore, blocks experiences of feeling nurtured, powerful, loving, and profoundly insightful.

For this reason, our sexual energy must express itself somehow. But when it's not released intentionally, the energy can come out in distorted ways that may be harmful. This energy gets distorted into two opposite sides and expresses itself in myriad ways on a continuum.

On one side, we find the sexual energy raging out of control, causing behaviors like obsession and addiction. This can be the husband who sneaks out of his bed to go watch porn all night long, and then can't focus at work the next day. It could be a young, urban woman who wakes up in a different stranger's bed each weekend feeling empty.

On the other side, we might attempt to gain control over the sexual energy, which results in more compulsive behaviors. This could take the form of sexual anorexia, where someone avoids all romantic relationships because they're afraid to lose control. Maybe a woman takes a vow of independence because deep down she feels inadequate if she does not look like the airbrushed models used to sell stuff or the idealized actresses in action movies. This could also be a man who, through an effort to be "spiritual," takes a vow of celibacy. While I'm not saying celibacy is a bad thing, it can often be used as a moral, high-ground excuse to avoid guilt, shame, and fear around sexuality.

In between those two extremes, I often see couples who are basically happy and have sex, but feel like something's missing. Can you relate?

Sexual energy must be experienced, understood, and channeled properly in order to master it. Then we can find a balance where we are neither repressed, nor out of control. This balance is the doorway to sacred sex.

FROM SEXUALLY TRANSMITTED DISEASES
TO SACRED ENERGETIC EXERCISE

We need a new understanding of sex, one that is beyond our definitions of physical pleasure, objectification, and repression. To truly heal our collective sexual wounding, this understanding must include spirit. When we bring sacred wisdom to our conception of sexuality, we can go from sexually transmitted diseases (STDs) to sacred energetic exercise (SEX). Then it becomes possible to see sex for what it truly is—an exchange of energies.

I refer to sex as a transaction of *prana*. Prana is our energy or life force. It takes many different forms, including our inhale, our exhale, even the words we speak or images we absorb through our eyes. Prana implies everything that you take into your being and all you release back into the world. Some forms of prana exchange are:

- Rain pouring on trees and flowers, resulting in growth
- Listening and speaking with someone with utter love
- A deep, warm hug between two people
- A kiss between lovers, friends, or child and parent

In all the above forms, some movement is interacting and giving birth to a new energy. Technically, anywhere an energy exchange takes place, some form of sex is happening. Now, I don't mean to tell you to go to a coffee shop and tell the barista that you want to have sex. Don't say that sex means exchanging energy between the coffee maker and the coffee drinker! I just want you to understand that we are taking in and giving out prana in every moment.

And sexual activity is one of the most potent pranic exchanges available to human beings. It holds the power of creation itself. Think about it. The exchange of genetic material can create an entire new life where there was no life before.

Like all things we take in or give out, this transaction can create nourishment, intimacy, closeness, and spiritual awakening. Or it can create anxiety, obsession, and shame. My point is this: We get to choose how we show up to our sexuality. If we desire to create something beautiful, meaningful, and oh-so-satisfying, we can.

In order to go from distortion to clarity, it is important to question everything we think we know about sex. We need to break the norms around sexuality that prevail in our culture. When we expose any false or limiting beliefs, our awareness will have the space to receive more evolved wisdom.

We can evolve our skills for managing our sexual energy. When we know how to use a machine, we can use it to be productive and progressive. When we don't understand its use, many things can go terribly wrong. Put a child behind the wheel of a car, and prepare to see a disaster. Give a criminal a gun, and watch what they do with it. A skilled driver knows how to operate a car properly. A police officer or soldier knows how to handle the incredible force and responsibility that comes with a gun. If you know how to use something the right way, you will employ its full power and create something good out of it.

Then we can be curious. We can work toward a more open acceptance of our sexual desires. That means acknowledging their presence but not reacting to our desires like untamed animals. Only then can we learn to respond mindfully to our sexual energy.

When we approach sex as a sacred energy exercise, we can bring about many revolutionary changes. Some of them may include:

- Reduction or a total end to rape
- Fewer sexual disorders
- Less sexual abuse
- No addiction to porn
- No objectification of gender
- Healthy intimate relationships

We can learn to greet the energy of the muladhara chakra with love—and channel it in an exalted way. We can meditate upon our desires and face them boldly. We can find a balance, where we are neither repressed nor out of control. This balance is the doorway to sacred sex.

Welcome to the rapture and ecstasy of divine love.

NORM 15

SEX IS FOR PHYSICAL PLEASURE ONLY

Everywhere we look in today's media-saturated landscape, we get the message that the reason to have sex is to feel physical pleasure. Sex is often seen as a mere friction that scratches an itch. Everyone is obsessed with the perfect orgasm: how to have one, give one, have multiple ones, find the best position, and so on. I find it interesting that the sex-toy industry has proved to be recession proof. And a friend sent me a text message saying that the first person to discover sex was probably just trying to create fire by rubbing together random things and then discovered that the same thing could happen with bodies. I find that comment humorously wise!

The problem with this collective fixation on physical gratification is that we don't see the bigger picture. When we are focused on this small aspect of sexuality, we miss the totality of the gift of sex. The mind hijacks the creative, loving, passionate, healing energy of sex and reduces it to a single-pointed goal. The result of such behavior can only be frustration, a feeling of never being fully satisfied. That's because our bodies and spirits long to connect intimately with our lovers and the divine. This is only possible through awakened sexuality.

BREAKTHROUGH

FROM KAMA SUTRA TO CALM SUTRA

Take a moment. Breathe deeply. Now, tell yourself that you are ready to see sex beyond just intercourse or friction. Really set an intention to move beyond the physical dimension of sex. Unless, and until, you are willing to understand sex beyond its usual parameters, this powerful transformation will elude you.

While I don't deny that sexual gratification is a pleasant aspect of the human experience—it is not the only story. When sex is practiced with the intention to experience truth and deepen our relationships, we touch the divine.

There is a beautiful Hindu tradition, which provides an inspiring way to think about sex. *Shaktipaat* translates as "the transferring of energies from master to student." The degree of shaktipaat varies from school to school. It could mean a spiritual initiation performed by a Guru. This often involves the Guru giving a seeker a mantra to work with in meditation, which yields specific results. It can also mean transferring special spiritual powers from an enlightened master to the one who will carry forward the lineage. It describes any experience of spiritual quickening or awakening that occurs when you meet a great being.

This exchange creates miracles. After receiving shaktipaat, students have been cured of illness, seen through limiting beliefs for the first time, and gone from disbelief in God to complete faith. That's because shaktipaat channels spiritual energy from the source of all life into an individual. This energy is the force that heals us. It blesses our lives in miraculous yet utterly natural ways. It's the power that holds us in complete love, and never lets us go.

It is a great blessing to receive shaktipaat from an enlightened master. This is often the easiest way to achieve boons in our spiritual practice. But it includes any transfer or exchange of energies. Shaktipaat certainly also takes place when a mother feeds her infant, for example. This concept can help us to evolve our understanding of sex, too. We can think of sex as a form of shaktipaat between lovers. Sex can be a practice where we invoke, receive, and share the movements of spiritual energy.

I'm not saying this process is ethereal and beyond the body. What makes it so satisfying is that shaktipaat takes place *in the body*. It is the transmission of spiritual energy from the unseen into the physical world. It can be a sacred gift we channel for our beloved, and our beloved channels it for us. Let me tell you, the bodily pleasure of exchanging love in this way is out of this world.

For these reasons, we have to be extremely careful about who we are sleeping with. The moment a kiss, a hug, or even a handshake is shared, an energy exchange takes place. When we sleep with random people or even with one person, we allow a significant exchange of energies between both parties. Loving a person of higher energy will help you feel fulfilled. Being with a person who carries anger and has a perverted mind will only lower your energy.

So mastering sex has nothing to do with learning complicated gymnastics or techniques. But if that brings you joy, more power to you! Evolving our sexual practice has everything to do with the meaning we choose to place upon it. It invites us to practice mindfulness on every level. With an intentional approach, sex can heal us, help us grow, and bring us closer to all of life. When we go from kama sutra to calm sutra, it's possible to feel fulfilled, joyful, relaxed, and overflowing with love.

EXERCISE **UNDERSTAND SHAKTIPAAT**

We can better understand the energetic exchange that takes place in shaktipaat by doing this practice in the presence of a tree. Eventually, try the same practice with your lover, first without touching and then during your physical, emotional, and spiritual union.

Choose a lush, healthy tree with plenty of greenery. Spend a few days to establish a connection with this tree. Shower it with water, talk to it, and become buddies with it.

After some time, sit under your tree. Take a few deep breaths. Visualize a circle of light around you. Spend a few moments on this visualization until you can feel the warm glow of your own light.

Then visualize the same light around the tree. Spend a few moments breathing with the tree. On every inhale, bring in the tree's light. On every exhale, give your light to the tree. If you like to work with mantras to help quiet the mind, you can silently say "Namaha" on the inhale, and "Shivaya" on the exhale.

NORM 16
WOMEN ARE
SEX OBJECTS

We have disconnected sex from divinity but connected it to everything else. Sex has been twisted and used as a tool to sell everything in the world. While watching a simple advertisement for soda, I noticed that the spokeswoman was half-dressed and quite turned on by her magical soft drink. This is just a subliminal message that connects that particular soda to a sexually attractive element. And the same message is given with many other products, such as perfumes, clothing, household products, cars, and even food. All the advertiser needs to do is simply flash an image of a half-naked man or woman on the screen to coax viewers into buying their product. It does manage to garner the attention of the viewers. Sad to say, but many yoga publications and spiritual magazines have resorted to doing the same thing to grab the attention of their readers by portraying yoginis scantily clad, with alluring looks on their faces.

No matter how much we have progressed, we still fall behind when it comes to giving equal respect to women. The objectification of women in art and movies is one example; I can go on and on. I spend most of my time in Los Angeles. The billboards all over Sunset Boulevard showing "100% nude girls" are just a representation of our ardent need to see women's bodies. The more I travel, the more I see how the bodies of women are being sold for just a few bucks but also for a high amount. But you simply cannot put a price on the divinity of women.

BREAKTHROUGH
WOMEN ARE THE
DIVINE FEMININE

Goddess worship is a common practice in India. If you travel there, you will see images of women representing various aspects of the divine. Some of these images show beautiful women dressed in silk and jewels, holding objects that represent spiritual bounty and fulfillment in each of their arms. Other goddesses are depicted as more ferocious. They can be shown trampling on dead bodies, wearing garlands of skulls around their necks. These images represent the death of limiting beliefs and egoic obstacles that keep us from knowing the truth of our divinity.

Religious devotees of both genders offer gifts and flowers to the goddesses as a form of prayer. They keep photos and statues of the Goddess in their homes, and ask her daily for blessings in their spiritual and worldly pursuits. Entire temples are dedicated to the abundant iterations of the divine feminine. I grew up learning that women are divinity personified. I was taught that if you break a woman's heart, then you break part of the universe, too.

So you see, India practices a form of objectification that is actually beneficial to the balance of masculine and feminine powers. The Western Judeo-Christian heritage misses this entire side of spiritual practice. But humans have a need for both aspects of godly representation to have a complete grasp of the divine's true nature. This need to see the female body with awe gets warped into the "Live Nude Girls" signs we see in every city. I don't claim that India or Hinduism has mastered the art of respecting women. Rape, domestic abuse, and objectification exist in India, but a huge chunk of the population is open to looking at women through a different lens. The first step is to create an understanding about women's beauty; other steps can follow. We can take our cues from the Goddess traditions before they were corrupted by masculine influence.

If we reclaim the gifts of the Goddess traditions, we can move beyond seeing women as sex objects. We can honor and love women as the glorious embodiments of spirit they are. In doing so, we open the doors to a new, more fulfilling sexuality.

KAMAKHYA: WORSHIPPING THE VAGINA AS YONI

I once read a quote by Swami Ramakrishna Paramhansa, the greatest worshipper of the Goddess Kaali. It said, "God is in the vagina."

That statement shook me initially, because one tends to associate spirituality with everything *but* the V-word. But in deeper study of this mystic man, you will see that his work expresses a deep reverence for the divine feminine principle as the source of love, life, and spirituality. Through him, we can learn to revere women's bodies as the divine's own expression.

The Kamakhya Temple in the Assam state of India is known as the abode of the Goddess Kamakhya. It is also known as *Yoni-Peeth. Yoni* literally means "vagina" and *peeth* means "home." So the temple is called "vagina home."

Legend has it that this temple was built in the location where the Goddess's vagina fell from the sky after an incident involving her husband, Lord Shiva. Parvati (also known as Kamakhya), wife of Lord Shiva, had gone to attend a ceremony organized by her father. Shiva was not invited to the family function, which angered Parvati.

Unable to take this disrespect to her godly husband, Parvati committed suicide by flying above the clouds and dissolving her body into fifty-one pieces. Her body parts were scattered into fifty-one different locations all over India. Each location later became an energy shrine to worship and to seek energy from her. Kamakhya is known as the place where her yoni fell.

Spiritual science claims that the yoni is the most important source of creation. Not only because it is the first and primary chakra of the body, but also because a woman brings new life from there. The Kamakhya Temple is a no-nonsense energy center for advanced seekers. I have been going there since my school days and witnessed sages whose mere presence demands respect. They don't talk much, but their eyes do a lot of talking. I was told to accompany a senior spiritual master during my first visit to the temple, so my father took me there and explained the whole science around it.

The shrine is dark with no light inside it as a way of showing respect to the Goddess inside. However, the most fascinating ritual is when the Goddess is believed to undergo her menstruation period once a year. During this menstruation time, the temple is closed for a few days. A white sheet of cloth covers the entire temple from inside. Consider it a sort of sanitary napkin for the Goddess. This is not the mystic part, by the way. The mystic part occurs when the temple doors are opened after those few days. The entire white sheet is turned into a reddish color.

While some people say it is the flow of the Goddess's menstrual blood, others say it is due to red vermillion powder in the water flowing through the temple. There has been no fixed explanation of this phenomenon.

The cloth is considered a source of miracles. To get even an inch of that cloth requires a good influential contact with the high priest of the temple. When I got mine, I was in eighth grade. My parents had it locked in a gold pendant, making sure it was safe and got its well-deserved respect. Even today, I keep it with me as a token of my respect for the Goddess's immense energy.

Can you imagine living in a culture where the vagina is honored as a source of blessings and giver of spiritual insight? Where women's images are used to explain the mysteries of the universe? Where men and women alike pray to her form each day, as a way to connect with the divine? When we learn the ways the Indian imagination has given meaning to women's bodies, it seems sad that other cultures view them as objects to sell beer and cars.

If you can travel to India to witness the temples and images I speak of here, I highly recommend it. But if you can't make the pilgrimage, you can still break the norm of sexual objectification. The following practice will help you to cultivate a daily experience of the divine feminine. You don't need to worry about how the practice will affect your sex life. I strongly feel that her loving energy will come into your being and create healing in ways you could not orchestrate yourself.

EXERCISE **BUILD YOUR RELATIONSHIP WITH THE DIVINE FEMININE**

Choose a goddess who appeals to you. You can select Kaali or Kamakhya. You can also choose any other feminine image that represents the divine for you. This can include a flowing river, a tiger, a blossoming flower, a goddess from another tradition, or a female body part.

Build an altar in your home that conveys the energy of the divine feminine as your imagination sees it. You can include pictures, objects found in nature, anything that makes you think of the Goddess when you look at it.

Light a candle for her each day. Making space in your day to honor her will create a positive change in your awareness.

Sit in front of your altar and meditate on her each day. Use whatever practice you like. Here is one suggestion that brings in the concept of shaktipaat from earlier in this chapter: Visualize taking the energy of the Goddess into your body with every inhalation. On every exhalation, imagine you are offering blessing back to her. Do this for twenty minutes.

NORM 17
SEX IS SEPARATE FROM GOD

I studied in a Catholic school until tenth grade. I often heard how sinful sex was. I almost looked at it as some sort of crime. I even felt I was born out of a criminal act. As young kids, we didn't understand much about our teachers' work as nuns. All we knew was that they weren't married.

Later on, when I realized how sacred nuns' jobs are, I wondered why my memories of them were of women who looked lifeless and dry. They were quick to anger and seemed joyless. I can say similar things about some Eastern monks who have taken a vow of celibacy. I have seen them getting frustrated over tiny things in the blink of a moment.

Of course, not all who take vows of celibacy are angry or frustrated. Taking such a vow is a huge thing, and one needs to be extremely connected with the divine to carry it out well. Sadly, that does not always happen.

In my speech class during college, I chose the topic "Catholic priests should be married." My argument was that if Catholic priests were married, there would be less child sexual abuse. During my research on the topic, I came across many stories of children who went through this painful trauma in the church. Religion creates such rigid formulas for finding God that it ends up making chaos in the already-disturbed human mind. The person taking a vow becomes too involved in keeping up the promise of celibacy that his compassion unconsciously turns into ego. That's why sex scandals often arise in the lives of those who had once taken a vow and then renounced it. With the vow, they had probably paused the deviancy. But once you repress the action, mental activity happens at double speed.

Sex is natural. Expressing it is natural, too. The problem is that many traditions teach a fundamental separation between the physical and the holy. That means the body, and all its processes, belongs to the realm of the earth, while God exists only in the heavens. When Eve takes a bite of the delicious apple, symbolizing physical desire and satisfaction, she falls from grace. In this line of thinking, it is necessary to transcend the body in order to reach spiritual insights. The body is a problem that must be conquered. Physical desires like hunger and sexual attraction must be tamed and the movement of the mind must be stilled. In this paradigm, only then can enlightenment happen.

Sex, then, is seen as a barrier to the divine. Relegated to the shadows, it is a shameful, dirty secret that leads to shame and guilt—a surefire way to create suffering. The sexual energy does not go away; it builds up and implodes in other areas of life, like outbursts of anger or physical illness or abuse that harms victims and perpetuates the collective shame around sexuality as a destructive force.

The belief that sex is separate from God is not exclusive to Western traditions. Many Eastern contemplative traditions preach celibacy as well. So do metaphysical subcultures. Consider the yogis who take vows of a *brahmacharya,* following a lifestyle of the divine. When interpreting their vows in a classical sense, brahmacharyas abstain from sex. They believe doing so will allow them to focus all their energy on spiritual practices instead. "Success" in meditation means they stop thoughts of sex and become so strong that they can turn off their sexual urges.

FROM CELIBATE MONK TO CELIBATE LOVER

Celibacy is an important practice to understand when it comes to sex and spirituality. This understanding plays a significant role in harnessing our energy in the highest and best manner. Most people associate celibacy with abstaining from sex completely. Every time I talk to my clients about sex and spirituality, they think I am going to ask them to become celibate and stop having sex. But I can't tell a fish to stop being in water. Some things are just not possible, and I certainly wouldn't want that karma in my consciousness.

On the spiritual path, it can be useful to become what I call a "celibate lover." We think celibacy means giving up sex, but it can simply mean practicing sexuality in a conscious way.

Celibacy is the English word for brahmacharya. Brahmacharya is a combination of two words: *brahma,* which means ultimate divine and higher consciousness, and *charya,* which refers to lifestyle or daily routine. So it means having a lifestyle of divine or higher consciousness. Being a celibate lover, therefore, is the commitment to bringing divine consciousness into sexuality.

Sexuality is creation. And creation is an important part of the divine. Any divine lifestyle won't require you to stop creating, but it will certainly expect you to evolve your methods of creating as you age. A celibate lover lives the moment so fully that they are no longer controlled by their sexual impulses. The creative impulse is transmuted into an experience of love and spiritual ecstasy.

This entire chapter is aimed at teaching you to become a celibate lover.

The suppression of sex is not celibacy. The expansion of sex into higher consciousness is celibacy. If you feel you are not ready for it, don't put on a pretentious show about elevating sex. Celibacy is also not fully practiced if you stay away from the opposite sex physically but, in your mind, you are undressing everything that moves. Doing these things will only misalign your chakras further.

As a celibate lover, live your desires so fully that you know the business of your every emotion. I recommend that you understand your inner self well. Get in touch with your sexual desires and emotional needs. Let your skin breathe when you want to, be playful with nature, and never repress your emotions. A meditation before or after the sexual act can help you experience higher states of consciousness. Before sex, a meditation relaxes you. During sex, a meditative mind helps you to experience the bliss moving and exchanging between partners. I recommend meditation after sex. You don't have to sit straight and chant mantras. Simply lie in bed and watch your breathing and awareness moving through your body. In this state of vulnerability, meditation takes on a beautiful movement. It will bring you to a state of security and love. Of course, the popular norm is to sleep, take a shower, or go home in certain cases. But if we have decided to go beyond the norms, meditation after sex is quite a powerful way to rewire our energies.

Many masters even suggest having a conscious sex practice with your partner. This can still be considered part of celibacy as long as it is practiced as a sacred energetic exchange in a clearly defined couple. Such couples tend to be spiritually inclined, best friends with each other, and guided by the divine in every moment.

BREAKTHROUGH
SEX IS AN EXPRESSION OF GOD

I invite you to live a life in which sexuality is not a barrier to the divine. What if your experience of sexuality expanded your awareness of God? What if it provided a doorway to know God immanently, as your own body, and at the same time, so much more? What if it opened your soul to greater love and connection with all that is?

With a shift in perspective, our sexual energy becomes a tool for greater awakening in our lives. When we start looking at sexual energy as divine, sex will become a divine act. The popular notion of "Change the way you look at things and the things you look at change" holds true in this case.

Consider this: The mere presence of sexual energy within us makes us divine. Without this powerful creative energy, nothing would exist. In that way, the creator and creation are not separate. God is not in the heavens, looking down at us and creating our lives. God lives within us as our vitality and creativity. It is our desire to be and to create that manifests as the world. And it's those desires that lead us to the divine. When we harness our sexuality with intention, any application of that energy becomes a spiritual practice. In India, this notion is more common than in the Western world.

EROTIC TEMPLES IN INDIA

The Khajuraho temple in Madhya Pradesh portrays the entirety of human life, including the erotic. Images of the deity, or God, can be found inside the temple walls, while the outside shows sculptures of people making love or participating in other daily activities of work, family life, and so on.

The symbolism here invokes the teaching that you have to cross the sexual in order to reach the divine. It teaches to move skillfully through the *kama* (sex) to reach the *rama* (divine). Sex and divine are not two separate phenomena here. They are interconnected.

The temples don't encourage sex. But they encourage us to understand it deeply because the path of the divine crosses through it. In this way, the aspects of our physicality are essential points on the spiritual path. We must work with these very human realities on our journeys to know spirit. The problem will occur only if we are stuck on the outside of the temple.

On my first wedding anniversary, I took my wife to the Khajuraho temple to just meditate on this mysticism. We spent two entire days simply looking at the art depicting an entire married life. The rocks are so alive that you can't help but start a conversation with each of them. We found that contemplating the temple art illuminated our relationship with one another as well as with the divine.

If we could build Khajuraho in every city of the world, we would have a healthy world to live in. There would be no more sexual perverts and no more rapes. It used to be a mandatory ritual for spiritual students to come and meditate in these temples. They were asked to meditate on erotic art in order to merge into it deeply. The idea was to have seekers face the sex drive and alchemize it into something higher.

For some students, that meant simply calming the sex drive down, while for others it meant channeling it to explore the meaning of existence, soul, and all queries of mind. A person in their twenties would be sent to these kinds of temples to understand the ocean of sexual energy within them. Can you imagine how different our culture would be if our young people participated in a rite of passage such as this?

Khajuraho happens to be a Tantra temple. As you can see, Tantra does include sexuality, but perhaps not in the way you thought. Next, let's move our discussion on to debunking misunderstandings that surround the Tantric tradition in the West.

TANTRA MAKES YOU A KING IN DIVINITY, NOT A KING IN BED

We owe a huge apology to Tantra for using it as a label for the practical skills in sex. Every time I Google "Tantra," countless images pop up of couples in various human and nonhuman lovemaking positions. Growing up among Tantra teachers from day one, it was almost impossible for me to believe what I was seeing. With a little more online browsing, I saw Tantra's name was incessantly used to promote various sex schools. It was like promoting laptops only as a typing machine. Sure, that's one of a laptop's features, but it has countless other functions as well.

I remember asking my spiritual Guru, my father, "Dad, did you train me to be a sex therapist?"

Embarrassed a bit, he politely replied, "No, not at all, son. Why do you ask?"

I had to share with him all the trash happening in the name of Tantra. His reply did soothe the questions I had.

"Marketing experts probably needed to make money for their clients. They picked up the most exploited element in the world, sex, and promoted it heavily using the label of Tantra. People crave love and better and more pleasurable sex, and they bought what was being sold to them."

So what is Tantra, then, if not a technique for better sex? It is a complete worldview, with myths, traditions, teachings, and practices to empower its followers. I see Tantra as a technique of self-realization, a path to higher consciousness, a method for experiencing enlightenment, a science of understanding soul business, and a tool to experience worldly and spiritual abundance. See how the Western marketers sell Tantra short?

Tantra attaches meditation to everything we do. In this sense, an experience of sexual attraction is not a barrier to our realization, but an invitation to practice awareness, intention, and skillful action. Our sexuality is not a problem to be solved, but a gift to be cherished and understood. There is no need for renunciation. We can be in the world, but not bound by its challenges. The "secret" is to simply be present in every moment. In the moment that we experience our humanness fully, without trying to stop it, we see our divinity.

Studying with a qualified Tantric is the opportunity of a lifetime to alter your consciousness. A qualified master can give you mantras and meditation techniques that will reveal your freedom within the boundaries of a human body. I highly recommend that you study with a master if one crosses your path.

If you cannot study with a master in person, the following practice will give you an introduction to Tantric sexuality practice.

EXERCISE **BREAK THE NORMS KAMA MEDITATION**

This is a brief introduction to the Break the Norms Kama meditation. The goal of this meditation is to help unblock sexual energy and channel it to serve your higher self. This meditation is taught under diligent supervision at the Break the Norms center. For the readers of this book, I am presenting beginner's instructions to get started. Please note that all meditations are best done with qualified guidance.

Yoni Mudra

As discussed in this chapter, yoni invokes "vagina" as a source of creative spiritual energy. *Mudra* means "posture." In this exercise, we will use a posture made with the hands to channel the flow of prana. This particular mudra is considered the highest state of mudra and is recommended for advanced seekers. I often get my clients to do this and have seen tremendous results.

I recommend doing this mudra after meditation. The symbolic meaning of this mudra is to birth a new you from the inside out, creating a new consciousness out of the yoni. Hence, the name Yoni Mudra is given to this sacred method.

The tips of our fingers are powerful transmitters and receivers of energy. In Yoni Mudra, you effectively transfer yourself to an empty space and redirect energy back into yourself through your hands. This mudra disconnects you from the senses of seeing, hearing, smelling, and speaking so your awareness can focus on aspects of the divine which cannot be accessed through the senses. To make the Yoni Mudra:

Cover your eyes with your middle and index fingers.

Cover your ears with your thumbs.

Cover your nostrils with your ring fingers. Move the fingers when breathing in through the nose. Breathe out through your nostrils.

Your pinky fingers rest gently on your chin.

Kama Meditation

Wear clean clothes. Light candle, incense, or *diya* (cotton thread dipped in clarified butter) to create good vibes around yourself. Sit with your spine erect. Watch all sensations in yourself without judgment.

This practice involves positioning your body in a mudra (sacred posture) to invoke specific energy. You will find the instructions for this mudra below, followed by the exercise instructions.

Bring all of your awareness to your breath.

After a few deep breaths, watch the stillness flowing in you.

Comfortably, bring your awareness to your muladhara chakra, located at the base of the spine between the anus and genitals.

Keep all the awareness on it for a few moments.

Repeat this affirmation silently to yourself: "I witness my sexual energy with no judgments." Continue to bring awareness and energy on muladhara.

Take up the Yoni Mudra effortlessly, with no force and absolutely no discomfort. Stay in this posture for no more than two minutes.

Then, keeping your eyes closed, remove your hands from your face and open your eyes. Look at your hands. Then proceed to rub your face and neck with your hands very gently.

As you feel comfortable, bring the energy flow to slow motion and then a complete halt.

WHAT ABOUT DEATH? 8

During the early morning hours of March 23, 1931, on the cusp of India's revolution against colonial rule, prison guards came into a young man's cell and told him to get in line. It was time to be hanged.

The young man, who was reading the biography of Lenin, smiled and said, "One minute, sir. One revolutionary is meeting another." Once he had finished the passage, the man put the book aside and walked with his two fellow cellmates toward the gallows. On their way, they sang a song which roughly translates as, "Oh, mother India, color my robe with your colors."

This is a true account of Bhagat Singh, a young revolutionary who fought for India's independence. According to the recorded accounts, as well as eyewitnesses, Singh had every opportunity to flee the scene where he was arrested. Instead, he chose to let himself be arrested and hanged, with the intention of inspiring India's youth.

I was born in the state of Punjab, the same region where Bhagat Singh was born. His heroic stories were part of my student life. His death certainly inspired me. Even after so many years, his name evokes respect and honor because of his bravery and how he chose to end the journey of his life. He chose to conclude his work with his death.

This chapter is not about patriotism or how to end your life at twenty-five. It is about the freedom that comes when we no longer fear death. Because he did not fear death, Singh was able to courageously offer his life to what he believed in, and choose a meaningful death. Each of us has the opportunity to be as fearless about death as Bhagat Singh.

CULTURE OF FEAR

In our culture, we have been conditioned to think of death as the worst thing that can happen in the course of a life. We are afraid of even the thought of death. In some cultures, there is a lot of crying expressed at the moment of death. Death is a taboo for so many of us.

In our day-to-day lives, we avoid thoughts of death at all costs, even while we fear the day it will claim us. Just look at the commercials on TV. They sell insurance to mitigate the risk of death, or pharmaceuticals promising to postpone our death. The message is clear: keep death away because death is bad and, therefore, scary. The youth are idolized. There are antiaging expos, creams, and many treatments that fight against age. I often wonder why anyone would want to antiage. I certainly want to age gracefully. Antiaging feels like an attack on nature's flow. You will never see a tree trying to reverse its age or a mountain trying to look young.

Aging has its beauty. I love talking to older people. It feels like reading classic novels wrapped up in old covers. It comforts me to talk to someone who has "been there and done that." Aging and death aren't tragedies. Our ignorance about death makes it a tragedy.

When we don't accept our eventual deaths, fear and panic lay beneath the surface of each moment. It's as if there's an elephant in the room that we are avoiding. We strive. We hope. We try to control our lives to create an illusion that we can escape death or, at the very least, postpone it. Every decision we make is laced with anxiety. That's because the fear of death underlies all fear. We may be conscious of a particular fear, an accident, a breakup, or any change. But if we have not yet faced the fact that our bodies, our minds, and our personalities will be lost, all fear is intensified by the ultimate fear, the fear of death.

We may lie awake at night, worrying about all the "bad" things that could happen. We may wonder if we will die in a few days, or a few months, or a few decades. Perhaps we feel regret around the life we might have lived if we were not so afraid. We may believe we need anti-anxiety medication to go on living.

But life does not have to be this way. This fear of death is a norm that we can break through. When we do, we can live courageous, free lives. Only when we accept death as an event as natural as birth are we free to truly *live*.

WHAT WE FEAR

Why do we fear death? We are afraid to walk in the dark because we can't see what's coming ahead. Yet, when lighted, the same path holds no fear for us. Simply by making the situation known, we are able to overcome our fear. The same is true for death. We are scared of death because we don't know what will happen to us once it arrives. No one is there to teach us about death because everyone relates to it with pain and sadness. We always relate to the deaths of others with shock and pain. If we think about our own deaths, it invokes pain.

We are conditioned to fear loss of any kind. We feel sick at the thought of losing our bodies, but that is not all. It's common to cling to everything we have. For example, during life, we are largely concerned with how to acquire wealth and, once we do, how to keep it. When I was studying finance in Manhattan, one of my professors told us about a rich person on the verge of dying. He called for his wife and asked about his sons.

"Where is Tom?"

She said, "He's sitting next to your feet praying to God."

"Where is John?" he asked.

"He is getting your medication," his wife replied.

"Where is David?" he asked about his third and youngest son.

"He's also here, honey. We are all with you!"

"Well, who's in the office then?"

Even at the moment of death, many people remain stuck in bank accounts and balance sheets. For many people, a significant aspect of their fear of death has to do with a concern over who will take care of all the wealth and business plans when they're gone.

And what about the fiery flames of hell? How many people feel tortured at the thought of ending up *there* after death? Or for those who believe in reincarnation, the fear of death coming back as a destitute laborer, or worse, as a slimy worm, can subconsciously persuade us to make wacky decisions. We buy the newest antiaging remedy. We marry someone who is "acceptable." We slave away just to contribute to a 401(k).

Can you see how our fear of death gets in the way of living?

DEATH'S TRUE NATURE

I remember the gut-wrenching train ride to the hospital where my sister had been admitted. When I arrived, I received the dreaded news that she had gone into a coma. She died a few days later. She was only nineteen years old, and her death was the hardest thing I had ever faced. I expected an older person to die, but not my sister. She was studying to be a doctor. She had her whole life ahead of her.

I felt completely lost. My faith was in crisis. But looking back, I can see that, though her death was tragic, it was also a moment of new learning. It forced me to make an inquiry into the meaning of life and death. I could either lie down and give up or accept her death. And in accepting her death, I accepted all death. This is the gift of facing death, however it shows up. When we seek to understand it, we can let go of our fear. I invite you to make this inquiry for yourself. My intention is to guide you through your own process by sharing my stories and discoveries.

I have realized this deeper truth about death: it is as natural and normal as birth. I am often asked if there is a way to conquer death, but my response has always been why do you want to conquer death? We "conquer" our enemies. Death is not something to be conquered. Believe it or not, death is not your enemy. It is actually a sacred and unavoidable phenomenon we can understand as an expected—even celebrated—event in life. Knowing that death is as natural as birth is liberating. Seeing deaths all around us should humble us that one day we'll die, too. And it is okay. What is born must die.

Death is a requirement for any living being. It is mandatory, and no one is exempt from it. Name one person you know who will not die, and

I shall change my attitude about death. Life is not guaranteed, but death is certainly guaranteed, so why stress about it? I don't mean to be flippant about this, but truly, every single one of us will die. Nothing we could ever do will change this fact. However, suffering in death is optional. Acceptance will end our suffering.

The key to acceptance is to understand what death actually *is*.

When airplanes were first invented, people must have wondered how this machine could fly all the way up in the sky and not fall. But with more knowledge about how it happens, flying at thirty-thousand feet while drinking a soda is not even a question anymore. Not everyone gets the science of flying airplanes, but flight is so commonly experienced in everyday life that most of us are at peace with it. In the same way, once we face and understand the process of death, there will be no more fear about it. We will just take it as it comes.

You see, in reality, death is a completely neutral event. Whatever meaning we place onto death is *up to us*. That means we can treat death with fear, resistance, and pain or we can treat it with curiosity, compassion, and even awe. Now that's real freedom.

How can we choose a more positive relationship with death? By breaking the norms, of course! This chapter lists three common cultural norms, which, once broken through, will open the doorway to fearlessness. Give it a try and see what happens.

NORM 18
WE ARE
OUR BODIES

Patients in hospitals are pronounced dead when a nurse or doctor confirms the absence of vital signs. That means as long as the heart is beating and the lungs are breathing, we exist.

But have you ever wondered if there is more to the story? Is life a purely scientific phenomenon? Is our existence related only to the physiological processes that can be explained in a medical journal?

If you are reading this book, I suspect you already have a hunch that our bodies are only a small fraction of our totality. But in our culture, we are largely taught to identify our bodies as *who we are.*

Upon waking, we think, "I am tired today" or "I am energized today," instead of thinking, "My body feels tired" or "My body has energy." We spend the day feeding our bodies, getting our bodies from point A to point B, and attending to our creaking knees or aching backs. On a good day, we feel the pleasure of sunshine on our faces or an embrace from a loved one. These experiences can certainly be poignant. But in this sense, being "alive" is only experienced at the mundane, physical level.

When we meditate or pursue any spiritual practice with sincerity, we have a chance to awaken to subtler, more sublime states of our existence. We have the opportunity to discover what is not made of cells or tissue, but of consciousness and bliss. We can have a direct experience of the spark that dances our hearts into being each day: the soul.

BЯEAKTHЯOUGH
WE ARE
LIMITLESS SOULS

A soul is what animates a body. It is our life force, our spiritual heart, and our connection to the infinite. It is made of awareness and unconditional love. Though as humans we experience our souls through our bodies, our souls are not exclusive to our bodies. Really, without soul, the body is nothing but junk. Just as your iPad doesn't do much without Wi-Fi, the body is empty without the soul. I don't deny that the body is important. It is indeed precious and very rightly considered the "temple" of your soul. But the body is not who we are. The soul is who we are.

And, although the body dies, the soul does not die.

The body is a vessel for our life force. When the body is lost, the life force simply moves to a different location. This process is similar to the way we shed identities and labels as we go through transitions within a lifetime. We are the same essence, constantly shifting and taking slightly different forms.

In a lifespan, we go from student to professional, single to married, childless to being a parent. These changes in identity can be easeful or they can be difficult. The problem has nothing to do with the changes themselves, but with our attachment to them.

When someone asks us who we are, we usually reply with our name, job, nationality, or marital status. This is the reason why we go through so much pain and anguish when one of these labels is snatched away, whether through disease, job loss, or divorce. We are conditioned to believe that our labels define who we are. When they are lost, we often feel that we do not exist. But just as the soul is not bound to the body, it is not subject to these labels, either. The soul exists in the realm of spirit. It is free. We could lose every single label, and *who we are* remains untouched by any loss, including death.

You see, the soul is limitless. While our embodied lives are largely subject to what our bodies can or cannot do, the life of our souls is unbound by any labels or limitations. This includes the body. While the body is limited by the cycles of death and birth, the soul is not. In reality, the soul has never been born and, therefore, does not die.

In our ignorance, we perceive that the material world is what's real. This is the root of all fear. When we endeavor to understand—and live from—our souls, we will not be afraid of death.

LOVE IS PROOF

Love exists in the soul realm. It's true that we can feel love when we slow dance with our beloved. We felt it when our mothers tucked us into bed at night as children. We feel it when our pets jump up and lick our hands when we walk in the door.

But if our beloved is at work, does our love for them go away? When we think back to our warmest childhood memories, do we stop loving our mothers? Do we stop loving our pets when we run errands? Of course not!

The same is true in death. Although the body disappears, the love does not disappear. When a loved one passes, we still feel the same amount of love—sometimes even more. That's because love is the soul.

And both love and the soul are limitless. They are immortal, unconditional, and not bound by the body. They are both *who we truly are,* in our essence.

Again, you should not take my word for it and "believe" you are a soul. The only way to gain the courage and freedom that comes from knowing your soul is to experience its presence for yourself.

YOUR SOUL DWELLS WITHIN YOU

One of the benefits of meditation is that it helps you to get a glimpse of your soul. In advanced stages of meditation, and of course, with the help of a qualified spiritual guide, seekers can have out-of-body experiences. During these higher stages of meditation, one tends to experience the soul as it is.

When experiencing the soul, you also experience how omnipresent it is. You realize that you are here, there, and everywhere. If I am leading a guided meditation for one person, a few people, or even hundreds of people, the most common feedback I get is that they saw their body meditating or they felt themselves *traveling* out of the body.

I am not a Buddha or a magician. What people experience is just their natural state of awareness. All I can do is prepare a soul with some warm-up exercises and then conduct a guided mantra meditation to bring people to such experiences. The ancient masters were spiritual Einsteins who created powerful, results-oriented methods to give a direct experience of divinity.

Meditation is a prerequisite for soul communication. Once you have a baseline of skill with meditation, you can ask your soul questions, and listen for its answers. When you have a direct experience with your eternal soul, you will know what does not die. Then there will be nothing to fear.

EXERCISE **Q&A WITH YOUR SOUL**

Have you ever wondered what you would ask your soul if you had the opportunity? You actually have this opportunity all the time. In meditation, you may effortlessly connect to your soul and ask any question. Another way is to write down a question on a piece of paper before you sleep. Or some people like to delve into these questions in the earliest hours of the morning when the sunrays are kissing the dewdrops on flowers. My experience says that once you start to devote time and attention to these questions, the universe also conspires to get you the information you requested.

For this exercise, simply pick one of the questions provided and meditate on it. You can come back to the same question as often as you wish, and pick a different question on a different day. You can also pick your own questions.

Do not ask questions to find some exact, specific answer. The aim is to meditate on the question with surrender and let the answers happen in their own way.

Take a comfortable seat. Close your eyes and breathe deeply. Take your awareness to your heart or the Third Eye (the space between your eyebrows), and gently ask the question.

Then let the question marinate within you. Don't try to get the answer. Remember, an answer is not the goal. The goal is to throw out the question; the answer will come when you are ready. Here are few questions that you may ask your soul:

Who am I?

In this question, your goal should be to find the roots of your existence. Who are you really? Find out for yourself. Keep posing the question, "Who am I?" You may not like what you see as the answer, but that's okay. The mind will give you many fancy answers. Especially if you have been in the "spiritual market" for a while, it will give you answers such as "You are a divine soul," "You are love," or "You are forgiveness." Reject all these answers. The ancient masters used the mantra *Neti Neti,* which means "neither this, nor that." Masters recommended rejecting all answers given by the mind. Only then will you see the layers peeling off to reveal a nonconceptual answer to the question.

What is the source of my happiness?

Let this question reveal only one answer: From where do you extract your happiness?

What is my source?

The question is simple. Ask your soul the source of your existence. You arrived through your mother, but your root source is somewhere deeper. Your mother was just a medium. There are many layers to your existence. What's a better reference to ask than your soul?

What is the meaning of life and death?

This is the most frequently asked question in all my talks. Everyone wants to know the meaning of life and death. Attendees ask me this question repeatedly. This is your chance to get your answer from within you—from your own soul.

NORM 19
DEATH IS THE END

If a loved one passes, we may assume that, because they can no longer sit at the kitchen table and drink chai with us, they cease to exist. That's because in our culture, we largely believe that death is the end. We don't have a context to teach us about what happens after death. We think we will never connect with our deceased loved ones again and fear losing the ones who are still alive. This belief often fuels the fear of our own death. Of course, death is very frightening if we believe that the short life in a body is all we have!

But death is not the end. Death is only a change in form.

I was raised Hindu, so my understanding of what happens after death has always been focused around reincarnation. I think of the body as a shirt that the soul puts on at birth and takes off at death. The body will keep on changing, but the soul remains forever. The soul has never died and, thus, has never been born. But the body gets the most attention because we are always indulging in it. We think that when the body dies, the soul dies, too. But as we discussed in the previous section, the soul is eternal. Therefore, death is only the soul "changing shirts."

All the world's religions offer explanations of what happens when this change in form happens. Christians believe that devoted practitioners go to heaven. Hindus believe in reincarnation. If you are curious to learn what different spiritual paths teach about life after death, I suggest you either read about every one or read about none at all. That way, you won't be held by any dogma. By reading all the literature on death across every culture, we will see that, although each spiritual path has a different vision, a common thread can be found throughout: death is not the end.

Of course, I would never recommend that you take my (or anyone's) word for it. The best way to realize that death is not the end is to experience it for yourself. Our loved ones can give us this experience when they pass. If we pray and meditate with the intention to connect with the souls of those we have lost, we often have a feeling that their essence is still available for contact. Though their bodies have died, their souls communicate with us. They reveal to us that the spirit does not end with death.

In India, it is common to contemplate the souls of our loved ones in this way. In fact, our culture includes rituals for families to make contact with those who have died immediately after the death happens. It is immensely valuable to process each death by establishing a post-death connection. Not only does it help us to feel peace after a loss, but it strengthens our faith that the soul does not die by giving us a direct experience of its eternal life.

BREAKTHROUGH
LOVE DOES NOT END

I'll never forget the day I was studying peacefully in my home in New York, when I received a phone call from India that changed everything.

"Ram was in an accident at the city's waterfall. His injuries were too severe. He died." I felt like I had been socked in the solar plexus. My cousin Ram was only twenty-two years old. How could he be gone?

Ram's death was a shock to my entire family, especially his mother. Auntie had three sons, but she was closest to Ram. He was the one who held the family together. He was the one who would care for his parents in their elder years. Auntie suddenly felt her entire family was lost, with no life-giving sun to hold them together in a logical orbit.

I saw my Auntie's despair and became very worried. It was as if her soul had left her body, too, even though she was still going through the motions of life—baking naan and balancing the checkbook. But she had no spark in her eyes. I prayed for a way to help her.

Then one night, my cousin came to me in a dream. He looked happy and young and told me he was doing very well. He asked me to tell his mother that he was fine. She did not need to worry. He needed her to accept his death.

The next morning I rushed to my Auntie to relay the message. She cried, and I could see her shoulders relax as her face became a bit brighter. Later that day, we visited a shrine where we meditated together for hours. We could both feel my cousin's presence with us. Through our prayer and openhearted awareness, we allowed the love we shared with Ram to touch us. This contact healed the pain of our shock and grief. We left the shrine feeling renewed.

After that day, my Auntie began to feel happiness again. Many external factors in her family life shifted in a positive direction. The family business took a turn for the better. Her other sons began spending more time at home. Best of all, Auntie's spark returned.

Of course, when a loved one dies, it breaks our hearts. We suffer the loss of a particular form. A life is a blessing. A life is a *life*. When it ends, grief is natural. But love does not end. At the temple with my Auntie, love was everywhere. It was alive—touching our skin, administering healing balm to the raw tissue in our chest cavities. And we felt very clearly that this love was *the same love* we shared with Ram when he was still in his body.

That's because love takes place between souls. The soul itself *is* love. Unconditional love. Neither love nor the soul ends—not even in death.

EXERCISE INQUIRING INTO DEATH

As I said earlier, it is imperative that you make the inquiry into what happens after death for yourself. No amount of dogma can make us believe. And the purpose of understanding what was never born and can never die is not to be a "good" religious follower. We endeavor to understand life after death so we no longer fear death. This exercise will help you seek wisdom so you can break through the norms of fear that keep so many of us from living our lives fully.

Create a quiet, comfortable meditation spot in your home. Place in your line of vision a photo of a loved one whom you have lost. You may also place any objects that have significance to you, like a shell from a beach where you spent time with your loved one, or a personal item that belonged to them.

Close your eyes and take time to breathe in and out until you feel centered.

Then, simply sit in meditation with the intention to experience the presence of this person. Do not try to force anything or think too much. Simply relax and allow your meditation to unfold.

Keep in mind that you may feel your loved one's presence in the moment you are seated, but you also may feel it when you are not expecting it. Just by sitting with the intention, you will put the desired outcome into motion.

It is also a common practice to start each day with a moment of gratitude and love for those who have passed away. It is believed that our acknowledgment not only gives them healing, but also opens the door of strength to us as well.

NORM **20**
WE GO TO HEAVEN OR HELL WHEN WE DIE

The other day I was driving on the highway where I saw a towering billboard that read something like, "The end is near. Jesus saves. Call 888-NOT-HELL." Okay, I don't remember the exact number to call, but I recall the message clearly: accept Jesus or you will burn in hell for all eternity. Yikes!

Each religion comes with its own beliefs for punishing and rewarding the dead. This often makes God look like a CEO with branches in every religion, staffed with highly competent "junior gods" who create records of every single act in our life. The system seems to be set up in such a way that human life is nothing but a span of years during which we must prove our worthiness. In this paradigm, we live to fear God—and life itself. We live our lives out of a fear of what will happen when we die.

But there is a secret that, once understood, obliterates any illusions of a punishing or rewarding God. The secret is this: both heaven and hell (and life itself) are constructs of our consciousness.

While this secret is recorded in the Vedic texts, it is free from dogma, religion, cultural norms, and threatening billboards! That's because consciousness is free. Your soul is free. And you are free to focus on hate and be miserable, or to focus on love and be happy. Whatever you focus on will become your experience. This is true whether you are alive, approaching death, or have transitioned from your current life into the afterlife.

But don't take my word for it. I can share my story and offer what I have discovered, but in the end, you are the only one who can recognize this truth in yourself.

YOUR DESTINY IS UP TO YOU

In India, astrologers are considered high authorities to consult when making life choices. Marriages are arranged around compatible charts. Business owners make major decisions based on "the stars." You get the idea.

When I once had my chart read, the astrologer told me "it was written" that I would be short-tempered and angry. That was my fate and there was nothing to be done about it. But I did not want to live a hostile life. I wanted peace, so I meditated.

I knew that deep spiritual work can change many outcomes that seem set in stone. When we strengthen our consciousness through practices, we are able to change patterns that have been in motion for years—even lifetimes. That's because we are constructs of our consciousness.

We can polish the quality of our internal world, and discover that our thoughts are malleable. We can direct the power of our awareness from a place of unconditional love. And wherever we place our attention becomes energized, whether we place it on anger and fear, or love and service. As I meditated, I burned through layers of frustration and anger. Now my internal and external life is mostly peaceful. Since my life is peaceful, I expect a peaceful death and afterlife. It is as simple as a river flowing in its course.

Here's a story to illustrate this concept: A child had been born to a renowned king in India. The king was told that his son would become either the biggest king this world has ever witnessed or a monk detached from worldly pursuits. The astrologers suggested, "If you want to make him a king, keep him away from all the misery."

As a result, the king constructed big mansions, each suitable for the season, and arranged that the most beautiful girls surrounded his son. The prince was shown only happiness, beauty, and longevity. One day, he was out and saw people taking a dead body to a funeral pyre. He didn't know what was happening, so out of curiosity, he asked everyone around. He was shocked to know that every human being grows old, falls sick, and ultimately dies.

Death appeared as his Guru in that moment. This detached him from the material pursuits, and he left the kingdom to find the meaning of life. This person is now known to us as the Buddha, the enlightened master we all love to love. He found his destiny on the very road that he was forced to take so that he could avoid this outcome.

In the same way, by focusing your intention and awareness, you can construct or rewire any aspect of your so-called destiny. And this destiny includes your mind-state when you die.

Have you ever noticed that when you are in a foul mood, cursing the traffic and the line at the grocery store, you always find more things around you to bring you down? It can seem like negative experiences come one after the other, and the world is against you everywhere you turn.

But if you sit quietly and meditate for a few minutes, I promise your day will change. Meditation buffs the dross from the surface of your thoughts and allows you to experience the spaciousness of your soul. Your soul is not moody, hostile, or impatient—it is unconditional love and awareness. When you connect with your soul, your perception shifts. And when your perception shifts, your entire world becomes brighter. You gain a sharper focus on what really matters. You realize you are free to choose your experience. So you see, your essence can choose your experience of life—and your experience of death.

We are co-creators in this game of life and death. You can partake in this game by consciously choosing and being aware, paying attention to every detail happening within you and around you. When we know this secret, there is nothing to fear.

BREAKTHROUGH
CHOOSE YOUR LIFE
(AND YOUR DEATH)

Anyone who wants to live in freedom will benefit greatly from realizing that our consciousness creates all experience—whether positive or negative. Basically, we are all going toward the same fate, which is death. The question is: How do we want to get there?

If we make decisions because we fear hell, we are not really living. Likewise, if we make decisions because we are trying to get to heaven, we are not free.

I've seen plenty of young lovers from dueling families separate because they believe that their marriage would displease God. Or what about two men who are in love, but fear that if they marry, they will go to hell? I think these examples show how we can waste the blessing of life because we are trying to avoid punishment after death.

The yogis in India are not afraid of heaven or hell. They are also not afraid to die. They live each day as a preparation for the final moment. Hence, they neither acquire much wealth nor hold on to grudges. During my visits to the Holy Ganges River in Haridwar, India, I have often seen many *Saadhus* (Indian saints) meditating in the river Ganges and peacefully leaving the body at their will. Don't believe it? Take the trip and see it with your own eyes.

I also have a YouTube video of myself sitting next to a Saadhu who tied himself with a blanket, to keep himself heavy probably following some ritual, and left his body. Some of them sit on a boat and peacefully leave the body. It is not suicide, as they don't take any drug or use any other means to kill themselves. They have such control over their minds and bodies that they can remove their souls when they wish to.

The concept of yogic death may almost seem like conquering death. But if you look deeply and with awareness, you'll see that the masters were never tempted to beat death. They simply wanted to travel to the next phase *as they desired.* The release of fear about death gave them enough freedom to live a life or death of their choosing.

It all comes down to choice. Someone once asked my grandfather what heaven and hell are. He replied, "When we are in the realization that we are divine beings, we are in heaven. When we are not in that realization, we are in hell."

His statement was enough for me to sail through this lifetime. I understand that he simply pointed at the power of choice we have in life. Based on this awareness, we live in many hells and heavens every day.

Hell happens when (but is not limited to):

- We are jealous
- We sow the seeds of hatred toward anyone
- Our intentions are not rooted in love
- We fall into the trap of anger
- We go on ego trips

Heaven happens when (but is not limited to):

- We become childlike again (but not childish)
- We are in a state of pure awareness
- We practice unconditional love
- We offer unconditional help to the needy
- We are in a joyful state

Therefore, what we think of as morality is not simply about "right" and "wrong," but about the experience we are creating for ourselves. We create blissful or horrible experiences during our lifetime, at our time of death, and after the death of our bodies.

BEYOND MORALITY

I am contributing some light to the concept of morality because it plays a deeper role in choosing your so-called heaven or hell. My take is that there is no such thing as "perfectly right" or "perfectly wrong" in the world. All morality codes are products of the human mind. We can act from lower states of awareness or higher states of awareness, but these acts themselves cannot be labeled as right or wrong.

I was born into a Hindu culture where you are told at the time of your marriage that if you even think of a woman other than your wife, you are committing a sinful act. At the same time, in the Muslim religion you are allowed to marry up to five women. What is normal in one culture is completely unacceptable in another culture. Morality is defined differently in different faiths. While I do feel there are universal wrongs—such as the tortures of rape, child abuse, killing as a form of punishment, marital abuse, and a few others on similar lines—it is difficult to label lifestyle choices as fundamentally either sinful or noble.

In my profession as a spiritual guide, multiple members of the same family confess their hearts to me and ask me to make a decision about who's right and who's wrong. Many times, all members are right. Their actions were right for their awareness. In the end, I always come to the same conclusion: that each person should work to raise their awareness and let the divine take care of actions.

Whether you reach heaven or hell after your death is completely your choice. It doesn't matter what you project to the outside world. If you feel within you that you have done something wrong and feel guilty, this becomes the foundation of your experience after death. There are people in the world who do charitable deeds because they believe that, if they are contributing to humanity, they will be rewarded in some way after death. Therefore, hell and heaven, just like life, are merely projections of our consciousness. So why wouldn't we choose heaven? Why wouldn't we choose thoughts and actions that raise our awareness and give us an experience of unconditional divine love?

There is no one employed by some higher CEO waiting for you to die so that they can decide what to do with you. The mysterious system of existence is more proficient than any well-run corporation. We simply get in return what we are investing.

WHY NOT CHOOSE HEAVEN?

I often wonder why we should even bother grappling with questions like this. Because when we no longer fear that we will end up in hell—when we no longer torture ourselves trying to be good so we can go to heaven—we have the opportunity to live a fearless life. We will have the freedom to love *who* we love, to love *what* we love. We can follow our hearts unconditionally. We can make choices that serve our soul's purpose. And we can know God intimately, without agenda.

Love and truth are the same. Truth is the all-pervasive consciousness. This truth is our inheritance, originating from our soul. Once a person gets a glimpse of this truth, all illusions shatter. It is this truth that breaks through cultural conditioning and our limited concepts of who we are. Truth softens hatred and allows us to forgive. It moves us to serve others. A heart that loves truth can bear any suffering or loss, including death.

When we realize this truth, birthing from our soul consciousness, life becomes fearless. And a fearless life leads to a fearless death. So why not focus on truth? On divine love? These are the forces that will liberate us from our conditioning. When we choose these aspects first, everything else works itself out. We have nothing to fear. We are free to *live*.

Now that sounds like heaven to me.

EXERCISE **MEDITATE ON YOUR INNER HEAVEN AND HELL**

I suggest you do this exercise in the early hours of morning
when your mind has not yet been bombarded with the demands
of the day.

Sit comfortably out in nature or somewhere peaceful wherever you are. On a piece of paper, write down the following questions:
- What is my definition of heaven?
- What is my definition of hell?
- Do I commit acts or make decisions based on my ideas of hell and heaven?

No need to write down the answers. Put your awareness on your heart. Feel it. Flow with it. Think about the questions that you have just written. Take the time to nonconceptually evolve into the answers on your own.

CONCLUSION

KEEP BREAKING
THE NORMS

How do you feel after reading the entire book? Maybe give it another read. Or pick the chapter that caused you the most discomfort. It's your call. Now that you have made it through your journey of breaking the norms, you have learned the importance of questioning everything you have been taught. You have discovered that listening to yourself above all else is the boldest spiritual act you can take. And you have learned that freedom and joy can be your reality.

On this journey, we have covered God and truth, life and death, sex and love. I hope that you have deeply explored what these topics mean to you. I hope you have a closer understanding of your own ego and the role it plays in your life. Most of all, I hope you have discovered greater clarity, peace, and purpose.

What you have learned in this book is just a warm-up for your consciousness. If your consciousness has been programmed in a certain way for many years, I don't expect it to rewire just by reading a book. Therefore, I invite you to reread the book after a gap of a few days or weeks and again apply the lessons from each chapter. Revisit the exercise from chapter 1. Then choose to read the chapter that resonates with you the most. The first reading was about getting acquainted with your norms. The second reading is when you will have "aha!" openings into higher awareness.

THE THREE I'S

It's important to realize that this work is a continuing process. Clarifying our consciousness is like taking a daily shower. We feel fresh, clear, and energized by taking the time to do our spiritual bathing each day.

To take the principles from this book into the world on a daily basis, I invite you to embrace the three I's:

Invoke the questions that arise in you after reading this book. Do not stop questioning. It is not by getting answers that you will find the truth, but by asking questions. Ask questions of your spiritual teachers, society, religion, government, and most important, yourself. The questions may annoy those who feel comforted by the norms. Don't accept the idea of life as lived by others. I don't want you to watch the singing and dancing of life. I want you to *become* the singing and dancing. Be the act of creation. That's your reality.

Invite your anger, desires, ego, attachments, and greed to be your friends. You cannot change an enemy. By treating these elements as your enemies, you look at them as obstacles—sinful and undesired parts of your existence. When you shift your perception, you develop a deeper understanding of your reality. You are no longer bound by society's definition of these elements. I want you to invite your deepest wounds and scars and meet them one on one. These elements are your bridge to move to the other side of their power over you. Many people choose to bypass this route and try to jump straight to the destination. A true norm-breaker understands that bypassing isn't an option.

Involve meditation in all your activities. Don't restrict meditation to just selective areas of your life. Meditation is not a separate part of your lifestyle. It is the *foundation* of your lifestyle. In addition to a dedicated meditation in the morning or at night, involve meditation at all times. Feel every chew of food, feel every drop of water while you shower, and when you hug, feel your complete being merged with another. I want you to be present and involved wherever you are.

Meditation is an important—perhaps the most important—tool in uncovering your most authentic life. Without meditation, this book does not have much meaning. With meditation, it holds power to alter your destiny. Therefore, meditate daily without any further delays.

NEXT STEPS

Once you have done the work of unlearning the norms that don't serve you anymore, the real fun begins! Then you can participate in the life you are meant to live with a fearless, pure heart. No longer bogged down by following a prescription for someone else, you have the freedom—and power—to create what your conscious desires dictate. This is what a life of purpose really means.

With this power comes the responsibility to apply yourself in ways that uplift and enrich spirit. You will realize that you can magnetize people and situations into your life. So make sure you know what you want to bring into your space! Meditation is the anchor that keeps you grounded and clear in your power. Come back to it moment after moment, day after day, week after week.

A PARTING REQUEST

Writing this book was a task that required a lot of responsibility on my part, as it was the first time that I shared the wisdom of my forefathers and my own spiritual journey on such an open platform. Now that it is out and I have poured my heart into it, I want to ask for your help in strengthening this thread further.

I would love for you to nominate any three people and ask them to break *their* conditioned norms, too. It can be any set of norms. Whether it's the aggressive way they drive, self-destructive eating habits, or avoiding meditation, the goal is to bring them onboard so that they, too, can gain awareness of their conditioned self. They can then nominate three more people to break their norms. The world around us is not living up to its fullest potential. Let's take this personally and help others to break the norms of conditioned collective consciousness.

Break the Norms has become a movement in its own way. What started out as a Facebook page is now reaching out to so many people through online groups and public events. One of the major missions of Break the Norms is to create meditation communities globally and help people break their norms. I highly encourage you to use this book as a guide to create meditation communities in your area. You don't have to be a certified meditation teacher or a new age yogi. You simply have to have a willingness to gather a community of seekers. You can find detailed information on this at BreakTheNorms.com. I hope you will be my tribe and join me in this mission.

ACKNOWLEDGMENTS

A vision and a hope, which started in my consciousness during my school years, took many journeys and turns. Now, finally it has manifested into a book. During the past few years, many inspirations walked into my life to support and encourage me to write this book, and I want to take this opportunity to express my gratitude.

I humbly acknowledge all the Gurus in the world, the masters who decode the mysteries of life. The great Gurus of the universe led me through intuitive guidance and used their "ways" to send me inspirations. I am just a medium. This is the voice of all masters who wanted us to question everything we think we know.

To my sister, Pooja, and best buddy, Abhishek, your passings shattered many illusions in my life. You both gave me a purpose for questioning life and death. Things would have been different if you were around. I miss you two.

To beloved Naana Ji, Daada Ji, and Daadi Maa. I feel your blessings, always.

Mom, your love constantly reminds me of all that is divine and beautiful in the world. May these writings reflect your amazing upbringing and values. Love you!

Thank you to my best friend, my truly better half, Rupali. Your presence inspires me to continue my mission in the world. I love you.

To His Holiness the Dalai Lama, your blessings manifested this book. I am so incredibly thankful to you for contributing the foreword. Your presence made this book so precious.

To Deepak Chopra Ji, your humbleness and wisdom are the foundations of my spiritual journey. The world will not see another Deepak Chopra. Your work will continue to shape many lives and inspire the generations to come.

To Mallika Chopra, you have been a great friend and guide. Knowing that I could always count on you for guidance helped me sail me through the process. I look forward to the unfolding of many of our intents to transform the world together.

To Georgy Bhaala Ji, yes! The book is finally out. Thank you for having faith and encouraging the writer in me.

To Sanjeev Sharda Ji, your efforts and support will motivate me for years to come. I am deeply thankful.

To Maureen Berrios, you saw why I am "here" and encouraged me to leave the financial industry for a better and higher purpose. I am so grateful to have you in my life.

To Merle English, thank you for acknowledging my columns in the college newspaper and for having the faith to spread my work all over. It was a turning point in my life.

To my schoolteachers at St. Joseph's Convent in Pathankot, India, and Baruch College in New York, I must confess that my obsession was the unfolding spiritual world always, but I am glad I continued my journey in school and college. It shaped me to better face the world. Thank you.

To my lifelines, who always treated me like a bestselling writer, even when I didn't know the ABCs of book writing. To our lifelong friendship! Thank you, my dearest Nikhil, Siddharth, Sahil, Jojo, Jaskaran, Gurbani, Megha, and Tripti. I love you all with my heart and soul.

To Kelly Notaras and Kate Sciolino, thank you for shaping my words and helping me to bring the book out in a much, much better way. This book wouldn't have been what it is without both of you. I am so grateful to have your energy behind me throughout the writing of this book.

To Bill Gladstone, thank you for being a fabulous agent and guide. I look forward to a great journey ahead with you.

Above all, to my fabulous publisher, Sounds True. I am incredibly thankful to Jennifer Brown and Tami Simon for acknowledging my message and giving me the opportunity to share it.

To Jennifer Holder, my editor at Sounds True, for her efforts to bring out my message so concisely. I will be forever grateful.

ABOUT THE AUTHOR

Chandresh Bhardwaj is a spiritual advisor and international speaker. Based in Los Angeles, Chandresh started his Break the Norms Movement with the intention to awaken human awareness from its conditioned self. He is a world traveler and gives talks all over the globe, including Europe, Asia, and North and South America.

Chandresh was born into a lineage of spiritual healers in India that has been enriching lives for more than seven generations. He combines this ancient wisdom with a modern approach to spirituality. Chandresh is a disciple of his father, His Holiness Shree Chamunda Swami, who is a universally recognized authority in Tantric spirituality. His grandfather gave him the name Chandresh, which means "Master of Consciousness."

Chandresh has long been fascinated by the incredible power of the inner self. At a very young age, he joined His Holiness Shree Chamunda Swami to visit various spiritual places in India where he would meditate under His guidance to seek the answers within. Chandresh strongly believes that the truth has to be realized from within. No one from the outside can tell us; we must discover the truth ourselves. Know more about his work at iamChandresh.com.

ABOUT SOUNDS TRUE

Sounds True is a multimedia publisher whose mission is to inspire and support personal transformation and spiritual awakening. Founded in 1985 and located in Boulder, Colorado, we work with many of the leading spiritual teachers, thinkers, healers, and visionary artists of our time. We strive with every title to preserve the essential "living wisdom" of the author or artist. It is our goal to create products that not only provide information to a reader or listener, but that also embody the quality of a wisdom transmission.

For those seeking genuine transformation, Sounds True is your trusted partner. At SoundsTrue.com you will find a wealth of free resources to support your journey, including exclusive weekly audio interviews, free downloads, interactive learning tools, and other special savings on all our titles.

To learn more, please visit SoundsTrue.com/freegifts or call us toll-free at 800-333-9185.